Training Laborers for His Harvest

Figure 1: Portrait of William Milne

Training Laborers for His Harvest

A Historical Study
of William Milne's Mentorship of Liang Fa

BAIYU ANDREW SONG

Foreword by Michael A. G. Haykin

WIPF & STOCK · Eugene, Oregon

TRAINING LABORERS FOR HIS HARVEST
A Historical Study of William Milne's Mentorship of Liang Fa

Copyright © 2015 Baiyu Andrew Song. All rights reserved. Except for brief quotations in critical publications or reviews, no part of this book may be reproduced in any manner without prior written permission from the publisher. Write: Permissions, Wipf and Stock Publishers, 199 W. 8th Ave., Suite 3, Eugene, OR 97401.

Wipf & Stock
An Imprint of Wipf and Stock Publishers
199 W. 8th Ave., Suite 3
Eugene, OR 97401

www.wipfandstock.com

ISBN 13: 978-1-4982-0707-2

Manufactured in the U.S.A.   03/11/2015

To my dear professors, mentors and friends,
Dr. Michael A. G. Haykin
and Rev. Keith M. Edwards

Then Jesus said to his disciples, "The harvest is plentiful, but the laborers are few; therefore pray earnestly to the Lord of the harvest to send out laborers into his harvest."

Matthew 9:37–38 (ESV)

Contents

List of Illustrations | viii
Foreword by Michael A. G. Haykin | ix
Preface | xi
Acknowledgments | xiii
Introduction | xv

1　Background to the Genesis of Protestantism in China | 1
2　The Making of China's First Evangelist | 16
3　The Theology of William Milne | 39
4　The Mentorship of Liang Fa | 58

Conclusion | 79

Appendix 1: Regulations Governing Foreign Trade Up To 1840 | 83
Appendix 2: To Pious Young Men | 85
Appendix 3: Memoir of Mrs. Milne | 89
Appendix 4: Works of William Milne | 102
Appendix 5: Works of Liang Fa | 105

Bibliography | 107

Illustrations

Figure 1: Portrait of William Milne | ii

Figure 2: Portrait of Robert Morrison
Painted by John Robert Wildman; Ref. 5871
© National Portrait Gallery, London | xxi

Figure 3: Portrait of William and Rachel Cowie Milne
From Townsend, *Robert Morrison* (1890) | 15

Figure 4: The Anglo-Chinese College | 38

Foreword

THE GROWTH OF THE Chinese Church in the last sixty years or so has been one of the great works of the Spirit of God in Church history. Yet, the roots of this movement of the Spirit go back well into the nineteenth century with missionaries like Robert Morrison, Hudson Taylor, and Lottie Moon . . . and William Milne—one of the forgotten pioneer missionaries of the Chinese Church. This new monograph on Milne and the first Chinese pastor Liang Fa is thus a welcome study indeed. The key role that Milne played as a pioneer of mission among the Chinese and his mentorship of Liang Fa has been done justice in this new examination by Baiyu Song. It is good to be reminded of such pioneers for theological reasons as well. For starters, reading of such men helps us never to forget the Holy Spirit's delight in using humanity to bestow grace upon later generations. Not only activities like baptism and the Lord's Table, prayer and preaching are means of grace, but men and women themselves as they live according to God's will. So Milne and his protégé Liang Fa were such means for later Chinese believers, even though they went unremembered. Well, at least unremembered till now.

Michael A. G. Haykin
The Southern Baptist Theological Seminary
February 2015

Preface

THE YEAR 2007 WAS the bicentennial of the arrival of Robert Morrison to China. It was also the year I left home and came to Canada. God loves irony: while my sister wished to study in Canada, and I wished to live in England, she ended up in Glasgow, Scotland, and I in Toronto. When I came to Toronto that October, I came as a high school student who was hurt, depressed, and lost. A few months before boarding the plane to Canada, I witnessed the death of my maternal grandmother on my birthday. This tragedy led me to reflect on the meaning of life. While I was attracted to the Christian faith, soon after I arrived Toronto, as a lay Buddhist monk, I started to read the gospel of Matthew and would later convert to Christ and attend a local church. Though I was aware of the celebration of Morrison's life that year, my thoughts were not knitted to the early Protestant missionaries until my second year of seminary studies.

In a private conversation with Dr. Michael A. G. Haykin, Professor of Church History and spirituality, Dr. Haykin, knowing my strong interest in history, encouraged me to research and focus on Chinese church history. With brief studies on the Nestorian missionaries, and a few modern Chinese pastors like Wang Mingdao and John Sung, I finally narrowed down my research to William Milne. When I first saw Milne's portrait, he reminded me of my deceased cousin. Thus, with personal curiosity, I spent few years of time on collecting books, journal articles, and other research materials on this remarkable man. In the summer of 2012, while

Preface

participating in a trip to England with a group of Southern Baptist Theological Seminary students, I was able access to the London Missionary Society archive in SOAS, University of London, and take pictures of some correspondences and journals of both Milne and Morrison. During that trip, I also visited the archives at Oxford University, where I made copies of Milne's published books in Chinese. In the University of Glasgow Archive, I found the senates' minutes of granting Milne an honorary Doctor of Divinity degree. As well, through Google Books, a few eighteenth century periodicals were made available for me to access.

In fall 2013, while I was a graduate student at Toronto Baptist Seminary, with prayers and encouragements from the Rev. Keith M. Edwards, the school's registrar, I was able to put my thoughts into a thesis, which was under the supervision of Dr. Haykin. While working on my thesis, Dr. Haykin helped and encouraged me to consider publication after I passed the oral defense. In the summer of 2014, I submitted my proposal to Wipf and Stock publishers, who considered my work and agreed to publication, which has become this present book.

Through setting to know and learn about Milne, I wrote this book in memory and appreciation of the foundational work of men like Morrison and Milne. Without this study, as a Chinese Christian, I would not get to know and understand my theological heritage. The New England theologian Joseph Bellamy once commented on Jonathan Edwards' published works, saying, "his aim . . . is not his own fame and reputation in the world; but the glory of God, and the advancement of the kingdom of his Redeemer." May this work, like Edwards,' also be for God's glory and his people's benefits.

Toronto, Ontario
December 2014

Acknowledgments

I CANNOT EXPRESS THE depth of my thanks for the support and encouragement of my thesis supervisor and now my employer, Dr. Michael A. G. Haykin, who in many ways is a spiritual father to me. Throughout the process of the writing and editing of this book, Professor Haykin modeled for me a godly, mature Christian scholar. I offer my sincere appreciation for the learning experience from Professor Haykin.

Thanks also are due to the librarians and archivists of the archive and special collection at SOAS library of University of London, Peter McGregor Memorial Library of Toronto Baptist Seminary, and the University archive of University of Glasgow. Without their help, I would not be able to complete this work.

I also wish to express my sincere gratitude to Principal Rev. Kirk M. Wellum; Rev. Keith M. Edwards; Rev. Haddon A. Haynes; pastor Glen M. and Professor Leah K. Zeidler; my uncle Gang Wang; and other friends, without whose encouragement and help, it would have been impossible for me to complete this work. Particular thanks are also due to the congregations of Richmond Hill Baptist Church (Richmond Hill, ON) and Lighthouse Bible Church (Don Mills, ON) for their encouragements and prayers.

I also want to thank and express my appreciation for my editors and friends at the Wipf and Stock publishers.

Above all I want to thank to my parents for their support during my five-year training at Toronto Baptist Seminary. With

Acknowledgments

gratitude and love, I pray for my parents that the Savior of Milne and their son would lead them to new birth.

Soli Deo Gloria.

Introduction

THE YEAR 2013 WAS the bicentennial of Adoniram (1788–1850) and Ann Judson's (1789–1826) arrival in Siam as its first Protestant (Baptist) missionary couple. While Baptists were celebrating this anniversary in remembrance of the Judsons, few people knew that July 4, 2013 was also the bicentennial of William and Rachel Milne's arrival in China as its second Protestant missionary couple. Today among Chinese Christians, very few know and understand the impact and influence this Scottish couple contributed to the church in China.

STATEMENT OF ARGUMENT

As noted above, William Milne (1785–1822) and Rachel Cowie Milne (1783–1819) were the second missionary couple sent by the London Missionary Society (LMS) to China, six years after the first Protestant missionary Robert Morrison's (1782–1834) arrival at Macao. It was due to religious and political persecution from the Roman Catholic bishops in Macao that Milne was forced to move and establish a mission station at Malacca. In his nine-year missionary business, Milne contributed greatly to the Chinese church by translating, evangelizing, preaching, teaching, writing, and mentoring. Though Milne only baptized two persons, Liang Fa (1789–1855) and a woman named Johanna, under Milne's influence Liang was led to conversion and later became China's first ordained evangelist. This book aims to explore how Milne led

Introduction

Liang to Christ through mentorship, and further helped Liang to become an evangelist.

STATUS QUAESTIONIS

Unlike contemporary missionaries, such as Judson, Carey, and Morrison, not many academic studies have been done on the life and work of William Milne, especially on Milne's mentorship of Liang. Soon after he passed away, the *American Baptist Magazine* published an article on Milne's death, since he was a significant figure in missions.[1] A year later (1824), Robert Morrison collected documents written by Milne and published *Memoirs of the Rev. William Milne* in English.[2] In this memoir, Morrison simply collected some of Milne's journals, correspondence, and his account of his life presented at his ordination. With very little editing or personal contribution (only a three-page preface), Morrison preserved most of Milne's writings in English.

In 1832, *The Chinese Repository* published a brief sketch of Milne's life and works as a missionary.[3] This article was the first brief biographical sketch of Milne's life and work. Due to certain limitations, this article, although excellent, lacked depth in the area of theological reflection. In 1840, Milne's close friend, Robert Philip (1791–1858), published Milne's first biography.[4] Since Philip had personally witnessed Milne's spiritual growth, he was able to provide some further information in addition to Morrison's *Memoirs*. Together with a detailed biographical sketch, Philip also analyzed Milne's theology (what he called "opinions") and missiology. Philip also included one of his own sermons preached to seminary students in London that encouraged them to become missionaries like Morrison and Milne. As time has passed, people

---

1. Anonymous, "Death of Dr. Milne," 109.
2. Morrison, *Memoirs*.
3. Bridgman, "Brief Sketch," 316–25.
4. Philip, *Life and Opinion*.

Introduction

have gradually lost their interest in Morrison and Milne, and Philip's *Life and Opinions* has stood as the last biography on Milne. In 1979, Brian Harrison published his *Waiting for China*, in which he gave a brief study of Milne with detailed accounts of the conflict with regard to leadership between William Milne, Walter Henry Medhurst (1796–1857) and Claudius Henry Thomsen (1782–?).[5] But as Harrison explained in his introduction, he had no interest in the missionary's pastoral ministry, and focused simply on the history of the Anglo-Chinese College in this work.

In the twenty-first century, there seems to be a renaissance of the study of early Protestant missionaries to China, but it is only the study of Robert Morrison that has occasioned any interest in Milne. Scholars like Christopher Hancock (St. Peter's, Oxford), Christopher Daily (SOAS, London), and Ching Su (Tsing Hua, Taiwan) have devoted works to Morrison.[6] Since one cannot study Morrison without Milne, in addition to these studies, Hancock, Daily, and Su have also included brief studies of Milne, which has made them the leading scholars today in Ultra-Ganges Mission studies.

From an academic perspective, there are still many aspects of Milne that need to be studied. Due to various factors, it was not until recently that Milne's genealogical information was discovered. For instance, work needs to be done on Milne's missiology, theology, ecclesiology, spirituality, marriage, his friendship

---

5. Su, *Open Up*. According to Su's research, Milne adopted and wanted to apply a "Chinese leadership model" in the missionary station, in which later missionaries would be under the leadership of the missionaries who came first. Since Morrison was in Macau, Milne became the leader of the Malacca station. This made the new missionaries, W. H. Medhurst and C. H. Thomsen, unhappy, and they complained to the LMS. Though Morrison stood with Milne and tried to explain the matter, the LMS made no further judgment, but required humility from both sides. As a result, Medhurst moved away from Malacca and established a new missionary station, and Thomsen moved to Singapore. This conflict directly led to the formation of the Ultra-Ganges Missionary Union.

6. Hancock, *Robert Morrison*. Daily, "From Gosport to Canton"; Daily, *Robert Morrison*; Su, "Printing Press."

Introduction

with Robert Morrison, his conflict with Medhurst, and theological roots (i.e., Milne as an Edwardsean).

PURPOSE OF THE CURRENT STUDY

First, this study is intended to be a remembrance of William Milne's arrival in China two hundred years ago, as well as his life and work there. As mentioned previously, there is not currently much interest in Milne in the academy and so this study aims to reintroduce Milne and his thought to academic studies, in order to encourage further work on this man of God.

Second, this study aims to argue for the biblical model of missions practiced by Milne in his mentorship of Liang Fa. Since the death of William Milne, there have been changes of missiology among missionaries to the Chinese. Ever since, there are questions about which missionary strategy or template should be used in China in order to effectively bring the Gospel to Chinese people. The classical debate is on the missiological approaches of J. Hudson Taylor (1832–1905) and Timothy Richard (1845–1919).[7] As the arguments go on, today some would suggest a "Sino-theology" model, which as a strategy tries to interpret and contextualize Christianity by Chinese culture, instead of the inspired Scriptures.[8] Such a model neglects the core message of the Christian faith, as its scholars are more interested in the academic value of Christianity, and lead it towards becoming a non-church movement. In today's China, the church by and large suffers from a lack of good biblical and reformed materials, but the most urgent issue in Chinese churches is rather the lack of theological foundations, that is, a lack of reformed pastors. A pastor is not merely a product of seminary training, or another educational institute, but is called and moulded by God through various means. Edward Smither, in

---

7. See Cohen, "Missionary Approaches," 29–62; Wong, "British Missionaries."

8. On Sino-theology see Kwok, "Moltmann's Method," 1–24; Lai, "Non-Church Movement," 87–103; Lai, "Sino-Theology," 266–81; Lai and Lam, "Retrospect," 1–17.

Introduction

a study of Augustine as a mentor, defines mentoring in the following way: "mentoring in essence means that a master, expert, or someone with significant experience is imparting knowledge and skill to a novice in an atmosphere of discipline, commitment, and accountability."[9] It is then essential to practice mentorship in order to produce reformed pastors who will be able to shepherd God's flock faithfully. This is the method Milne used with Liang. Through this historical study of Milne's mentorship of Liang, this writer hopes to examine the significant role of Milne's mentorship in the process of Liang's conversion and pastoral commission. Nevertheless, though space is not available for arguing the application of Milne's mentorship method in today's churches and missionary agencies, it is wished that through this paper, mentorship--the long forgotten missiological method--would recapture the interest of today's churches and parachurch organizations.

METHODOLOGY

Before presenting the methodology of this study, it must first be stated what this study is not. First of all, this study is not a biography of William Milne and Liang Fa. Neither is it a biblical reflection on mentorship, nor is it an essay on Milne's pastoral role. Rather, this study aims to examine the life and works of William Milne and to bring Milne back into his time and historical context, and evaluate whether or not mentorship was the best method of missionary endeavor at the time. In chapter 1, the general historical and sociological background of imperial China will be presented in brief. Though prior to Robert Morrison and William Milne, the Nestorian and Roman Catholic missionaries came to China and established churches in China under the emperors' permission and supervision, and yet Christianity had not taken root in China. Throughout the chapter, serious problems of contextualization, gospel communication and indigenization will be looked at in both Nestorian and Roman Catholic missiological methodologies.

---

9. Smither, *Augustine as Mentor*, 4.

Introduction

Meanwhile, in the eighteenth century, Protestant churches experienced the Great Awakening. This inspired the vision foreign mission rediscovered by men like Andrew Fuller, William Carey, and John Ryland, Jr., who later formed the Baptist Missionary Society for Promoting the Good News of Jesus Christ Among the Heathens. This Baptist-led missionary movement inspired the English Paedo-baptists, who later formed the London Missionary Society. It was through the LMS that Robert Morrison was sent to China, as China's first Protestant missionary.

Chapter 2 focuses specifically on Milne's life and that of Liang Fa. Chapter 3 explores the theology of Milne. Chapter 4 is on the mentorship, in which Milne's *Dialogues Between Chang and Yuen* will be analyzed in order to explore the way Milne led Liang to Christ, as well as to understand how Milne mentored Liang and taught him to communicate and evangelize his fellow Chinese. This will lead to the conclusion that as Morrison and Milne's primary goal was seeking Chinese conversions, and that mentorship was the most effective missiological method used in their historical setting.

Figure 2: Portrait of Robert Morrison
Painted by John Robert Wildman; Ref. 5871
© National Portrait Gallery, London

1

Background to the Genesis of Protestantism in China

JOHN FEA HAS ARGUED in his book, *Why Study History*, that the discipline of history is an "art of reconstructing the past."¹ In other words, the best historians are storytellers. As part of the construction of William Milne's story, this chapter aims to paint the larger picture of the historical, social, cultural and spiritual backgrounds of the two different worlds in which William Milne and Liang Fa lived and will lay a foundation for understanding details of the lives and thought of Milne and Liang in their historical setting.

THE SOCIAL AND POLITICAL STRUCTURE IN IMPERIAL CHINA

Sinologist Charles O. Hucker divided Chinese history into three epochs: a formative age (from the Xiao dynasty, 2205?–1766? BC to the Qin dynasty, 221–207 BC), an early imperial age (from the Western Han dynasty, 202 BC–AD 9 to the five dynasties era, AD 907–960), and a later imperial age (from Sung dynasty,

---

1. Fea, *Why Study History*, 3.

Training Laborers for His Harvest

960–1127, to the Republic of China, mid-nineteenth century).[2] During the Spring and Autumn (722–481 BC) and the Warring States (403–221 BC) periods in the formative age, different schools of philosophical thought rose, and each school tried hard to gain support from different kings. Though Confucianism, Taoism, and Legalism were the three major schools during this period, historically this era of cultural and intellectual expansion is both unique and significant for Chinese history, and was later called by Sinologists, "the Contention of a Hundred Schools of Thought."[3] Though China's first Emperor Qin Shi Huang (259–210 BC) persecuted the Confucian school (213–210 BC), in what historically is called "the Burning of Books and Burying of Scholars," Confucianism was not wiped out.[4] In 134 BC, Emperor Wu of Han (156–87 BC) took advice from the scholar Dong Zhongshu (179–104 BC) and made Confucianism the official orthodoxy by both nominating government officials from the Confucian school and using Confucian classics in bureaucratic examinations. From the Han dynasty on, Confucianism became the essential doctrine in China's worldview, even though during the later imperial age, China was controlled twice by tributary tribes of "the Inner Asian Zone," who were the Mongols (established Yuan dynasty) and the Manchurians (established Qing dynasty).[5] Moreover, one of the reasons

---

2. Hucker, *China's Imperial Past*, 1, 434–35.

3. For further studies done on this cultural and intellectual phenomena see Hucker, *China's Imperial Past*, 67–95; Bodde, "State and Empire," 1:72–80; Hu, "Comparative Studies," 83–95.

4. Aiming to re-unite the chaotic diversity caused by the Spring and Autumn and Warring States periods, Qin Shi Huang economically united the units of measurement (such as weight, measures, and currency), politically re-divided the administrative divisions, and intellectually combined the writing style of Chinese characters. Furthermore, as for intellectual thoughts, Qin Shi Huang took advice from Li Si (280–208 BC), his prime minister, and followed the Legalism of Guan Zhong (725–645 BC), which "concentrates single-mindedly on what must be done to make the state prosper and by survive--and ultimately to unite China." The "Burning of Books and Burying of Scholars" was a reaction by the emperor to his intellectual opponents, mainly from the Confucian school. Hucker, *China's Imperial Past*, 92.

5. Sinologist John K. Fairbank has argued that China's theory of

Background to the Genesis of Protestantism in China

Emperor Wu and the later emperors chose to praise and practice Confucianism was not that Confucianism held to a better teaching than the other schools of thought, but rather that Confucianism taught the common citizens to obey, to "follow and emulate a truly benevolent ruler."[6] At the same time, such teaching also satisfied the emperor's narcissistic needs as the emperor was thought to be the "Son of Heaven, who eventually became omnicompetent, functioning as military leader, administrator, judge, high priest, philosophical sage, arbiter of taste, and patron of art and letters, all in one."[7] Under such teaching, all religions in China became a means of state control and were used by the emperors to rule over their citizens. Thus, syncretism in China is not purely a religious matter. Interestingly, both the sociologist C. K. Yang and church historian Jonathan Chao argue for the continuity of the pattern of state control of religions from imperial China to socialist China. In other words, the same state order has continued to be practiced for more than 1500 years in China.[8]

The East India Company and Christian Missionaries

Beginning as early as the fifteenth century, "the Age of Discovery" was marked by the rise of colonialism, led by the Spanish and Portuguese. Not until a century later did countries like Great Britain and France start their global expansion. The East India Company

---

Sinocentrism was based on Confucian teachings about "family and social order, the official examination system, and the imperial Chinese monarchy and bureaucracy," which had directly influenced the "Chinese culture area," and China's foreign relations towards countries in three main areas, namely (1) the Sinic Zone, "consisting of the closest and culturally-similar tributaries;" (2) the Inner Asian Zone, including "tributary tribes and states of the nomadic or semi-nomadic peoples;" and (3) the Outer Zone, "consisting of the 'outer barbarians' generally, at a further distance over land or sea." Fairbank, "China's World Order," 14–20.

6. Hucker, *China's Imperial Past*, 79.
7. Fairbank, "China's World Order," 16.
8. Yang, *Religion in Chinese Society*, 180–217; Chao, "Church and State," vii–xxxiv.

(EIC) was founded in 1600, under the permission of Queen Elizabeth I (r. 1558–1603). It was primarily a private international trading company importing tea, sugar and various spices, and exporting goods including saltpeter. Yet, the EIC is unique among other trading companies, in that the EIC had a private army and was jointly owned by the British government. Under the support of the state, the EIC benefited from a colonial monopoly, military expansion in India, and the opium trade in China, which caused two Opium Wars between Britain and China after China's ban on the opium trade.[9] In contrast to the other European companies, which were a means for colonial effort and went hand-in-hand with Roman Catholic missions to the indigenous people, the EIC banned Christian missionaries from evangelizing in the colonies until the British parliament passed the Charter Act of 1813.[10]

Anglo-Chinese Relationship During the Qing Dynasty

China's world order is totally different from a Western world order because of the different mindsets, communication, and trade between China and the Western world (particularly with the British) that was unequal and uneasy from the beginning. "The Chinese World was hierarchic and anti-egalitarian,"[11] but for the British,

---

9. Editorial, "The East India Company."

10. Before 1813, missionary works were banned in India by the EIC. This policy was made in order to avoid any disruption that could be made by evangelizing the Christian gospel to the Indians who were already being diverse in their faith and culture. William Carey (1761–1834) and the other Serampore Trio members suffered under such limitations. Back in England, John Scott Waring (1747–1819) and Thomas Twining (1776–1861) openly opposed Christian missionaries in India by bring false accusation against Carey's mission. As a response, Andrew Fuller (1754–1815) published *An Apology for the late Christian missions to India*, and spoke with Lord Buckinghamshire (1760–1816), which directly influenced William Wilberforce (1759–1833) and Charles Grant (1746–1823), who worked as members in the Parliament to shepherd the passing of the Charter Act of 1813. See Farrer, *William Carey*, 52–58; Carey Study Center, "Charter Act of 1813"; Sunshine, "William Carey (1761–1834)."

11. Fairbank, "China's World Order," 16.

Background to the Genesis of Protestantism in China

"they understood that trade benefited both seller and buyer, who were like two lovers, each depending on the other for satisfactions neither could provide singly."[12] Thus, it is no surprise that there were later conflicts between these two worlds, for instance, in the Kowtow Controversy.[13] Due to pressure from the EIC, and the realization of the need for foreign trade, Emperor Kangxi (1654–1722) carefully opened Canton as the only location for foreign trade in 1685 and established the Thirteen Factories in 1686.[14] This was the first reopening of foreign trade since Emperor Hongwu of the Ming dynasty banned all foreign maritime shipping in 1371. Even so, the Qing government made strict regulations for the foreign traders to follow in Canton.[15]

Since one of the EIC's major trades to China was opium, later socialist historians accuse the British traders and missionaries of bringing opium to China. However, Chinese scholar Zheng Yangwen has noted that opium was first imported from Malacca and traded officially by the Chinese, and it was fashionable among the upper classes to smoke opium, which was seen as a luxury, "like tea drinking, was [part of their] material life and biological behavior, . . . and a culture of consumption."[16] Zheng states that the EIC were "cleverer than alchemists," since, by trading opium, Britain would

12. Peyrefitte, *Immobile Empire*, xix.

13. Alain Peyrefitte in *Immobile Empire* observed that misunderstanding and mistakes had been committed in early Anglo-Chinese relations during the three visits of British ambassador George Macartney (1737–1806) surrounding the kowtow issues, which Macartney had refused as he believed if he practiced kowtow before the Chinese emperor, it would mean the British king was subject to a Chinese emperor. This kowtow issue greatly concerned the Chinese emperor Qian Long, who wrote a letter to King George III in 1793. The whole letter had been translated into English, and can be found at "Modern History Sourcebook: Qian Long: Letter to George III, 1793," Fordham University, http://www.fordham.edu/halsall/mod/1793qianlong.html (assessed on October 29, 2013). *Kowtow* means "to kneel and touch the forehead to the ground in token of homage or deep respect."

14. Han, "Historical Status of Sup Sam Hung," 61–64. For detailed information on the Thirteen Faculties, see Milne, "Annals of Canton," 280–85.

15. See Appendix 1: Regulations Governing Foreign Trade Up To 1840.

16. Zheng, *Social Life of Opium*, 3, 43–44.

not only be enriched so as to build an expensive global empire, but also would "deplete China and hasten the downfall of the Qing dynasty."[17] EIC's trade increased the supply of opium. Thus, the common people in society were able to share the upper class taste, which for the upper class was intolerable. Therefore, Zheng argued that it was imperative for the ruler to ban opium, not for the purpose of morality, but for political reasons to keep the Chinese world order, and, for the rulers, it was expedient to blame the EIC traders.[18] As the MP and oriental diplomat, George Thomas Stauton (1781–1859), argued,

> The question with regard to the opium was not a question of morality or policy, but a question whether there had been any breach of international law. For a time, certainly, when the laws against opium trade were in a state of obeyance: when the viceroy of Canton gave the use of his own vessel to bring up the opium to Canton, they could not feel surprised that foreigners did not feel themselves bound very strictly to obey the edicts of the government...[19]

Such confusion and misunderstanding eventually led to the two Opium Wars (1839–1842, 1856–1860) between Britain and China and still impacts China (e.g., in Hong Kong).

NESTORIAN AND ROMAN CATHOLIC MISSIONARIES IN CHINA

Christianity as a general term is not new for the Chinese, since Christianity was arguably brought into China three times. Though without literary evidence, some surviving sculptures suggest that the apostle Thomas brought the gospel to China via India during the reign of Emperor Mingdi (*c.* AD 57–75) of the Later Han

---

17. Ibid., 56.
18. Ibid., 71–100.
19. Peyrefitte, *Immobile Empire*, xxxi.

dynasty, yet this view is controversial.[20] The first recorded attempt by Christian missionaries was by the Nestorians during the reign of Emperor Taizong of the Tang dynasty (626–648). According to the Nestorian Stele--which is now to be found in Xi'an Beilin Museum, Xi'an--on July 638, Nestorian monk Aluoben, bishop of Daqin, which "vaguely [refers to] countries of the west, probably meaning Persia or Syria, or even the Roman empire."[21] Aluoben was welcomed by prime minister Fang Xuanling (579–648) and introduced to Emperor Taizong. After hearing a brief presentation of Nestorian doctrine and being presented with a cross and Nestorian literature, Emperor Taizong gave permission for Nestorianism to spread and establish a Nestorian temple in the capital (now Xi'an).[22] With the help of the Emperor, *The Sutra of Jesus the Messiah* was completed, which was China's first Christian book.[23] In order to contextualize their writings, the Nestorians borrowed a lot of terms from both Buddhism and Confucianism in order to translate Christian literature into Chinese, and, in practice, the Nestorians lived in a manner very similar to adherents of Buddhism and Confucianism.[24] This practice of contextualization attracted some Chinese interests and eventually made thousands of converts, but when the Great Anti-Buddhist Persecution led by Emperor Wuzong (814–846) reached its height in 845, Nestorianism was wiped out as a branch of Buddhism. Not until 1271, when the Mongols conquered the Song dynasty, which was 426 years later, were the Nestorians brought back to China.[25] Although historically, the Roman Catholic Church condemned Nestorius and the Nestorians as heretics because of their doctrine that sepa-

20. This view is currently held by Roman Catholic scholars, see Perrier and Walter, *Thomas Fonde L'Eglise*; Daniel H. Bays had a brief survey on this Thomas-in-China view in Bays, *A New History*, 5–6.

21. Ibid., 7.

22. Eccles and Lieu, "Da Qin Jing," 2–5; also see Saeki, *Nestorian Documents*.

23. Tiedemann, "China and Its Neighbours," 369. A recent reprint is, Riegert and Moore, *Lost Sutras of Jesus*.

24. Lau, "Cross and the Lotus," 85–99.

25. By this time, many Mongolian tribes had been converted to Nestorian church. See Bays, *A New History*, 11–12.

rated Christ into two persons, divine and human, the controversy between Nestorius and Cyril of Alexandria was not purely doctrinal.[26] Martin Luther, Richard Baxter, and later William Milne, defended Nestorius as a Patristic reformer against the doctrine of *Theotokos*.[27]

The second attempt to introduce Christianity to China was led by missionaries from the Dominicans, the Franciscans, and the Jesuits from the Roman Catholic Church. In 1245, a Franciscan friar, John of Piano Carpini (1182–1252), carried two letters from Pope Innocent IV (c. 1195–1254) to Kublai Khan (1215–1294), seeking to convert him in order to make him an ally with the Roman Catholic Church against the Muslims. Though failing his mission, John of Piano Carpini built a relationship with emperors of the Yuan dynasty (1271–1368) and prepared the way for further Franciscans, such as Willem van Rubroek (c. 1220–c. 1293) and John of Monte Corvino (1247–1328).[28] These Catholics converted a number of Chinese, but most of them were Nestorians. Toward the end of the Yuan dynasty, the Roman Catholic Church's missionary attempts were halted due to the Black Death, the "Great Schism," as well as wars with the Muslims.[29]

Thirty years after the death of Francis Xavier (1506–1552), who was the co-founder of the Jesuits and missionary to Japan, Malacca and some Chinese, Matteo Ricci (1552–1610) a Jesuit scholar and linguist, arrived in Macau and later went to the Ming dynasty's capital, Beijing. Aiming to reach Chinese intellectuals,

---

26. For correspondence between Nestorius, Cyril of Alexandria, and Pope Leo I, see Norris, *Christological Controversy*, 123–59; McGrath, *Christian Theology Reader*, 260–82; Grudem, *Systematic Theology*, 555; also see chapter 3 "Christology" in Aprem, *Nestorian Theology*, 24–105.

Scholars argued that behind the theological conflict there was a political issue of Pulcheria, who directed Cyril of Alexandria to stand against Nestorius in defense of her political benefits as the emperor's sister and the virgin-like Mary. See Limberis, *Divine Heiress*.

27. McGrath, *Christian Theology Reader*, 280–82; Philip, *Life and Opinion*, 389–422.

28. Hill, *Zondervan Handbook*, 301–02.

29. Brief summary of Roman Catholic mission in Yuan dynasty and their conflict with the Nestorians, see Clark, *Church in China*, 16–23.

Background to the Genesis of Protestantism in China

Ricci adopted Chinese clothing fashion and became a Confucian scholar.[30] Although Ricci converted thousands of Chinese, and even the Prime Minister Xu Guangqi (1562–1633), Ricci and the later Roman Catholic missionaries failed to reach the commoners, due to their targeting of officials and intellectuals, and playing politics. This prevented the gospel's engagement of the common culture in common language. Also, due to their relationship to Rome, in 1704, the "Rites Controversy" between Popes Clement XI and XIV, and Emperor Kangxi of the Qing dynasty forced to ban Christianity in 1721 in order to protect Confucianism as the society's orthodoxy.[31]

THE LONDON MISSIONARY SOCIETY AND ROBERT MORRISON'S EARLY MISSIONARY IN CHINA

As a response to Arminianism, High-Calvinism was popular in the eighteenth century among the Calvinists, who believed that "the unconverted had no duty to repent and believe the gospel," and "[t]hat total depravity rendered them incapable of doing so without the regenerating influence of the Holy Spirit."[32] The eighteenth-century Baptist theologian, Andrew Fuller (1754–1815), and his friend William Carey (1761–1834), defended the faith by establishing the Baptist Missionary Society (BMS) with the support of like-minded Baptist pastors such as John Ryland, Jr. (1753–1825) and Samuel Pearce (1766–1799). On October 2, 1792, at Kettering, Northamptonshire, William Carey and medical missionary John Thomas (1757–1801) were commissioned as the BMS' first mis-

30. Jonathan D. Spence observed that Ricci tried to reach out to the Chinese by teaching his method of memorization and hoped the Chinese would ask from there about his God. Spence, *Memory Palace*. Also see Ricci, *On Friendship*, 1–82.

31. Brief study on the Rites Controversy can be found in Bays, *A New History*, 28–32; Rule, "Chinese Rites Controversy," 2–8; Mungello, *Chinese Rites Controversy*.

32. Modern, "Andrew Fuller," 2. Distinguishing between Calvinism and High-Calvinism can be found in, Nettles, *By His Grace*, 423–29.

Training Laborers for His Harvest

sionaries to India, and they set sail to India on March 20, 1793.[33] This marks the beginning of a new epoch in Christian global missions; in Richard Lovett's words, "the honour of leading the van in the formation of the great modern missionary agencies . . . belong to . . . the glory of the Baptist Church."[34]

In July 1794, Ryland received a letter from Carey regarding his first six weeks of missions in Bengal. Soon after Ryland finished the letter, desirous to spread the joy of Carey's missions, he shared the letter with David Bogue of Gosport (1750–1825) and James Steven (1761–1824), minister of the Scottish Church, Covent Garden, London, who were in Bristol for "the purpose of preaching special sermons at Whitefield's Tabernacle."[35] After they met with Ryland, Bogue, Steven, and John Hey (1758–1809), the minister at Castle Green Chapel in Bristol, met in the parlor of Whitefield's Tabernacle, which was then located in Penn street, and they prayed for "consultation on the best way in which they could arouse the public mind to the grievously neglected duty of attempting to send the Gospel to the heathen."[36] In the same year, Melville Horne (c. 1761–1841) published *Letters on Missions: Addressed to the Protestant Ministers of the British Churches*, in which he argued that British Protestants needed "to unite in a common missionary enterprise."[37] Thomas Haweis (1734–1820), the Principal Trustee of Selina Hastings, the Countess of Huntington (1707–1791), along with a group of paedobaptist Protestants, who had a common vision "to spread the knowledge of Christ among heathen and other unenlightened nations,"[38] established the London Missionary Society in 1795. In September, Bogue published an essay, "To the Evangelical Dissenters who Practise Infant Baptism" in the *Evangelical Magazine* (established in 1793), in which he "urged his

---

33. Haykin, "A Dull Flint"; Haykin, "Just Before Judson," 9–30; Andrew Fuller's apology for Carey's missions see, Mordon, "Andrew Fuller," 237–55.

34. Lovett, *London Missionary Society*, 1:4.

35. Ibid., 1:5.

36. Ibid.

37. Stanley, "Horne, Melville," 304.

38. Daily, *Robert Morrison*, 21.

Background to the Genesis of Protestantism in China

evangelical peers to engage in missionary work in India like that of Carey" and which also recommended the formation of a seminary to train a pool of twenty or thirty men to begin the work.[39] In the same year of its formation, LMS focused on the South Seas and sent their first missionary Thomas Haweis (1733–1820), to Tahiti, but due to their inexperience, the Tahiti mission failed. The directors of LMS did not realize their error until their missionaries also failed in the second missionary station, South Africa. The directors then found it necessary to change their missiological method.[40] By doing so, the LMS directors decided to take Bogue's suggestion to train men with sufficient mission knowledge, before sending them to the mission field. Therefore, at the beginning of 1800, the board of LMS decided to make Bogue's Gosport Academy their training center.[41]

As the LMS sought to establish a new missionary station, Bogue became interested in China, as he said, "three converts in China, . . . are worth twenty in Otaheite, and 500 in England with respect to the advancement of the kingdom of Christ among men."[42] Bogue identified Robert Morrison (1782–1834) in his Gosport Academy as the best candidate to be China's first missionary.

Robert Morrison was born on January 5, 1782, at Buller's Green, Morpeth, Northumberland, to James Morrison (c. 1740–1812), a Scottish farmer, and Hannah Nicholson (d. 1802), an English woman. Both were active members in the Church of Scotland. As a shy, sensitive and serious youth, Morrison recalled his conversion in an application letter to Hoxton Academy in 1802. He was influenced by the Evangelical Revival and grew to be aware that his "somewhat loose and profane life deserved God's judgment. He sought God's forgiveness and gift of 'life' through

---

39. Ibid., 45.

40. See Ibid., 21–35.

41. Daily argued that Morrison and Milne's missionary approach was rooted in David Bogue's vision, which was programed in the Gosport Academy curriculum. Detailed discussion on Bogue's curriculum can be found in Daily, "From Gosport to Canton"; Daily, *Robert Morrison*, 37–82.

42. Ibid., 84.

Training Laborers for His Harvest

Christ's atoning death," which led to a life change.[43] After his conversion, Morrison had a great love of learning, which was motived by his love of souls, and this led him to apply to study at Hoxton Academy under the tutorship of George Collision (1772–1847) in London.[44] Two years after his acceptance in Hoxton, Morrison joined Wells Street Chapel and received pastoral mentorship from Alexander Waugh (1770–1849). Though his tutors discouraged Morrison from any further theological studies, he was convinced and applied for an interview at the LMS on May 27, 1804. The next day, the LMS committee approved Morrison's application and sent him immediately to Gosport for missionary training.

In Gosport, after discovering Morrison's gifts, Bogue introduced Morrison to William Willis Moseley (b. 1781), who was burdened with a missionary zeal and was enthusiastically translating the Bible into Chinese, but Moseley had no interest in translating the Bible by himself.[45] With Moseley's help, a Chinese man named Yong Saam Tak, who desired to study the English language, was made Morrison's Chinese tutor. Yong moved in with Morrison on October 8, 1805, and tutored Morrison in Chinese, while Morrison taught him English.[46] For Morrison, the tutorship was not easy, since Yong was a "bright, educated, young man, with his strong opinions and fiery temper."[47] About the same time, Morrison studied the unfinished Chinese New Testament translation by Catholic missionary Jean Basset (1662–1707) then archived at the British Museum, which had been discovered by Moseley.[48] Morrison also discovered two Latin-Chinese dictionaries in the library of the Royal Society.

---

43. Hancock, *Robert Morrison*, 11–12.
44. Morrison, *Memoirs*, 1:21, 30, 31.
45. Daily, *Robert Morrison*, 86–91.
46. Ibid., 93.
47. Hancock writes, "When Morrison disposed of a scrap of paper Yong Sam Tak had written on, he took umbrage, for three days refusing to teach. A tin plate replaced paper to avoid a repetition. Yong Sam Tak modeled the elitist rigour of the trained Chinese mind . . ." Hancock, *Robert Morrison*, 26.
48. On Basset's New Testament, see Daily, *Robert Morrison*, 217, n. 40.

Background to the Genesis of Protestantism in China

In addition to Morrison's preparation for Chinese missions, he also went for medical, astronomical and geographical training with a Scottish medical student-cum-evangelist, William Brown.[49] On January 8, 1807, at Bogue's request, Morrison was ordained in the Scots Church on Swallow Street in London. On January 31, due to the EIC's anti-missionary policy, Morrison had to sail to New York first, and from there he had to seek aid and protection from the Americans in order to enter China. Morrison arrived in New York on April 20 and came under the American Counsel's protection. Morrison boarded the *Trident* on May 12, setting sail for Macao.[50] After a 113-day's voyage, the *Trident* anchored in Macao on September 4, 1807. William Milne later wrote about Morrison's arrival at Macao as

> having never been in foreign parts before, and being a perfect stranger to every one in the place; knowing also the jealousy of the Chinese, and the bigotry of certain Europeans, he had not the most encouraging prospect before him. Confiding, however, in the mercy and gracious Providence of God, he was not depressed.[51]

Three days later, however, Morrison was expelled by the Roman Catholic authorities in Macao, and he sailed to Canton, which was eighty miles up river from Macao.[52] Though lonely and living in a poor environment, with the fear of persecution by Chinese

---

49. William Brown was a "medical student-cum-Evangelist from Leith, Edinburgh," selected by the LMS through the Gosport Academy as the second missionary to China accompanying Robert Morrison. The LMS board spent money on Brown in order for him to receive sufficient medical and scientific knowledge, but in a letter he wrote to the missionary board on April 12, 1806, Brown resigned from the China Mission, citing his "unhappy relationship with Morrison as his main reason for withdrawal." Daily, *Robert Morrison*, 94, 95, 96–97.

50. Hancock, *Robert Morrison*, 33–35.

51. Milne, *Retrospect*, 63.

52. Peyrefitte observed in his book, "during the French Revolution and the Napoleonic wars, Portugal was Britain's ally. But the Portuguese missionaries in China were fervent opponents of the English, whom they considered 'arrogant miscreants.'" Peyrefitte, *Immobile Empire*, xxiii–xxiv.

Training Laborers for His Harvest

authorities, Morrison spent his time mastering Chinese. Later that same year, because of Morrison's unique ability in both the Chinese language and knowledge in "the proprieties and customs of Chinese culture," Morrison was hired by the EIC as a translator and later served as a linguistic and cultural assistant to Lord Amherst (1819) and Lord Napier (1834), when they visited the Qing Emperors in Beijing.[53]

At this stage of Morrison's mission in China, the LMS directors worried if Morrison would damage the mission due to a cultural clash with the indigenous people, as previous missionaries had done in their mission fields. Thus, they only viewed his mission as "a preliminary endeavor" and "instructed him to make no attempt to preach the Gospel openly."[54] Rather, the directors instructed Morrison to devote his time to studying the Chinese language and translating the Bible and Christian literature to help future missionaries.[55]

In 1808, Morrison went back to Macao for a physical retreat and was able to stay at Macao this time because of his employment with the EIC. Early the next year, the 24-year-old Morrison met the then 17-year-old Mary Morton and married her on February 20, 1809. For Morrison, although he had Mary as a companion-helper, he still felt lonely in the missionary field. He needed a friend and helper in this hard labor in a strange land. As early as April 29, 1807, Morrison wrote to the LMS directors requesting sending another missionary to China.[56] Though the LMS accepted Morrison's request, it took six years for the LMS to send William and Rachel Cowie Milne to China.

---

53. Rowold, "Robert Morrison," 106.

54. Barnett, "Silent Evangelism," 288.

55. During this period, Morrison finished the translation of New Testament in Chinese, and published it in 1813. Morrison also wrote and published two tracts in Chinese including, 神道論贖救世總說真本 ("A True and Summary Statement of the Divine Doctrine, Concerning the Redemption of the World." 6 leaves, Canton, 1811), and 問答淺注耶穌教法 ("An Easy Explanation of the Doctrine of Jesus, in Question and Answer." 30 leaves, Canton, 1812). See, Wylie, *Memorials of Protestant Missionaries*, 4–5.

56. Hancock, *Robert Morrison*, 88–90.

Figure 3: Portrait of William and Rachel Cowie Milne
From Townsend, *Robert Morrison* (1890)

2

The Making of China's First Evangelist

> Judge not the Lord by feeble sense,
> But trust Him for His grace;
> Behind a frowning providence
> He hides a smiling face.
> His purposes will ripen fast,
> Unfolding every hour;
> The bud may have a bitter taste,
> But sweet will be the flower.[1]

FROM A SWEARING SHEPHERD BOY TO CHRIST'S AMBASSADOR

William Milne was born in April 1785 (possibly on April 26 or 27) at Braeside of Cults, in the parish of Kennethmount, Aberdeenshire, Scotland, and was baptized on April 27, 1785.[2] Milne's father,

---

1. Cowper, "Light Shining," 295.
2. Based on Morrison's *Memoirs*, Su Ching argues that Milne was born in the parish of "Henethmont," instead of Kennethmont (See Su, *Open Up, China!*, 130, n. 2). Though the name "Henethmont" was used in Morrison's *Memoirs* (2), according to Milne's first biographer, Robert Philip, Milne was

The Making of China's First Evangelist

William Milne, Sr., who was a farm laborer, died when Milne was six years old (1791), and his "mother gave [him] the education common to others in the same condition of life."³ Possibly the oldest child and the only son, Milne had to work as a shepherd boy at a very young age. During this period of his life, Milne learned and started to swear while shepherding the sheep; later he comments that "the natural depravity of my heart began very soon to [discover] itself" and this led him into many other sins, like "lying, swearing, and blaspheming God's holy name."⁴ As Milne grew up in the parish church, he memorized *The Westminster Shorter Catechism* (1647) and John Willison's (1680–1750) *Mother's Catechism* in order for him to "be equal with [his] neighbours, and avoid the displeasure of the minister of parish."⁵ For Milne, "religion was

---

born in the parish of Kennethmont, where Philip himself grew up (*Life and Opinion*, 1, 5, 42, 65, 116). Su argues for Morrison's spelling, since he said that "Henethmont" appeared in Milne's application to LMS, but Su did not cite the reference of this application. I would argue that it was in the parish of Kennethmont that Milne was born. Morrison's "Milne's Account of Himself" was originally published as a tract, entitled *The Ordination Services of the Rev[erend] William Milne and the Rev[erend] George Thom; Missionaries to the East 1812*. In the preface of this document, its editor explained that this is a record of Milne's ordination service, which means this document was not in a written form where Milne gave his account of himself, rather this document was stenographically reported. I would argue that since the letters "K" and "H" are very similar, it is possible for both the reporter and editors to make a mistake in confusing "K" with an "H." Historically, according to Scotland Places (http://www.scotlandsplaces.gov.uk/), there is no parish named "Henethmont" in Scotland. Geographically, Kennethmont is few miles away from Huntly, where Milne attended church. Therefore, it is certain that Milne was born in the parish of Kennethmount, Aberdeenshire.

According to the discovery of a file entitled as "O.P.R. Births 212/0000100227 Kennethmont" in the Old Parish Registers from ScotlandsPeople (http://www.scotlandspeople.gov.uk), William Milne was born to William Milne, Sr. in Braeside of Cults, and was baptized at the parish church on April 27, 1785. The entire entry is "April 27—Milne, William in Braeside of Cults had a son baptized, named William—3 [shillings]." Withngton, *Old Parochial Regs*, 12, 02C186. In a journal entry dated on April 27, 1820, Milne wrote, "This is, so far as I have learnt, my birth day." Morrison, *Memoirs*, 84.

3. Ibid., 2.
4. Morrison, *Memoirs*, 2; Philip, *Life and Opinion*, 7.
5. Ibid. The full title of John Willison's catechism is *The Mother's Catechism*

very grievous."[6] As Milne later recorded, he once foolishly imagined that, by the age of sixteen, he would "attain great celebrity as a vain and trifling youth."[7]

According to Milne's account, by the age of ten, once walking alone at noon between two corn fields, his heart was awakened by reflecting on the idea of eternal punishment and hell. Such reflection made Milne horrified, and as a result, he made vows and dispositions about spiritual matters; but these impressions did not move Milne to Christ and were soon forgotten. When Milne was thirteen, God used various means to draw Milne closer to the cross.[8] What happened to Milne at this time, both physically and spiritually, brought Milne to attend Sunday evening schools taught by George Cowie (1749–1806). In the Sunday schools, Milne's knowledge of the Scriptures increased but this made him very proud. This pride led him to search the Scriptures, to pray, and hold prayer meetings with his sisters and other children. As Milne later claimed, all that he had done at the time was based on his self-righteousness, since he felt no need of Christ.

By the age of sixteen, Milne had left his mother and moved into another house, whose owners Milne described as "strangers

---

for the Young Child; or a Preparatory Help for the Young and Ignorant.

6. Philip, *Life and Opinion*, 7.

7. Morrison, *Memoirs*, 3; Philip, *Life and Opinion*, 8.

8. Milne described the means God used as: (1) reading of religious books, including John Willison's *Treatise Concerning the Sanctification of the Lord's Day* (1712/3), and *Seven Sermons on Different Important Subjects* (first published in early 1690s, and soon reprinted in the colonies) by Robert Russel of Wadhurst, Sussex; (2) the pious examples of two Christians who Milne lived with for a period of time. One of these two persons is an Adam Sievwright, who was a basket maker and who taught Milne making baskets. By Philip's description, this Sievwright introduced Milne to Christ, as he always talked with his "melting tones of his gentle voice," "seated amidst his bundles" of willows, "twisting a butter-basket, and talking about the glories of the Covenant of Grace to young Milne." (Philip, *Life and Opinion*, 20–21); (3) Milne's secret hope of being saved by his prayers, which made him proud and self-confident; (4) the fear of evil, and an experience of almost drowning in a small river, and (5) the sacraments of the Lord's Supper, where Milne saw the representations of Christ's suffering. Morrison, *Memoirs*, 3–4; Philip, *Life and Opinion*, 8–9.

The Making of China's First Evangelist

to religion."[9] But during this time, Milne visited a poor Christian man's house frequently.[10] In this house, Milne was first introduced to family worship, and as Milne joined with prayers, he was taught and encouraged to pray and read pious books.[11] Milne later recalled:

> From this time my enjoyment and pursuit of pleasure in the world were marred; and a beauty and excellence discovered in religion, which I had never seen in any past period of my life, and which led me to choose and follow after it as the only object deserving the chief attention of an immortal creature.[12]

With this awakening experience, there were two books that deeply shaped Milne's spiritual life: a book entitled *The Cloud of Witnesses* (1714) and Thomas Boston's (1676–1732) *Human Nature in Its Fourfold State*.[13] As Milne was eagerly seeking the salvation of Jesus Christ, two sermons moved Milne forward to conversion: Thomas Boston's published sermon, "The Soul's Espousals to Christ" (2 Cor 11:2), and George Cowie's sermon on Revelation 22:21.[14] Milne was then led to reason:

---

9. Morrison, *Memoirs*, 5.

10. Robert Philip in *Life and Opinion* states that he was not able to identify which family Milne stayed at the time and referred to here. Philip, *Life and Opinion*, 12.

11. Robert Philip records that when at the poor man's place, Milne always went "the sheep-cote, because he would have been disturbed in the barn, by his fellow-servants; and he carried a turf with him to kneel upon, because the floor was foul as well as damp," and prayed. It started there that Milne became a man of prayer. Philip, *Life and Opinion*, 13.

12. Morrison, *Memoirs*, 5; Philip, *Life and Opinion*, 13.

13. The full title of *The Cloud of Witnesses* is *A Cloud of Witnesses for the Royal Prerogatives of Jesus Christ; Or, the Last Speeches and Testimonies of Those Who Have Suffered for the Truth in Scotland, Since the Year 1680*. It is a collection of "the narratives of the sufferings of the Covenanters was resolved upon by the society people in 1699." Johnston, *Treasury*, 394.

14. Milne in his account, named Thomas Boston's sermon as "The Believer's Espousals to Christ," which should be "The Soul's Espousals to Christ," according to Samuel M'Millan's *Complete Works of Thomas Boston*. Philip, *Life and Opinion*, 16; Morrison, *Memoirs*, 8. M'Millian, *Complete Works*, 4:22–31.

If pardon and salvation were offered, "without money and without price," to those who had killed the Prince of Life, and thereby committed the greatest possible crime; then, surely that grace which could triumph over all their guilt, and so richly abound where sins of the highest aggravation once abounded, may be extended to me--pardon my sins, and renew my nature--heal and save my soul. By these two things I was led to discover a glory and suitableness in the Gospel--as displaying the lustre of the divine perfections, and as preserving the honours of the divine law, while at the same time it conferred eternal life on the guilty sinner believing in Jesus. This discovery captivated my heart, and made me willing to devote myself, soul and body, to God for ever.[15]

By having such "earnest desire of devoting [himself] to God," Milne was encouraged, possibly by either George Cowie or Adam Sievwright, to make a personal confession, which took place at "a place surrounded by hills on every side."[16] When making his personal confession, Milne "professed to choose the Lord as [his] God, Father, Saviour, and everlasting portion; and to offer up [himself] to his service, to be ruled, sanctified, and saved by him."[17] This conversion experience was accompanied with radical changes in his lifestyle, as Robert Morrison, Milne's missionary colleague, said about Milne's character after Milne's death. In Morrison's words, Milne had a "very ardent impetuous determined mind; yet softened by mildness of manner," and after Milne's conversion, "it retained its natural ardor and impetuosity, but [was] directed to new and very different objects from what it previously was."[18] According to Robert Philip (1791–1858), Milne also became a man of prayer after his conversion, which made his piety something admired among his fellow believers.[19]

---

15. Philip, *Life and Opinion*, 16–17.
16. Ibid., 17.
17. Ibid.
18. Morrison, *Memoirs*, iii.
19. Philip, *Life and Opinion*, 23–26

The Making of China's First Evangelist

Soon after Milne's conversion, he felt it necessary to leave the Church of Scotland, as he disliked the shallow sermons preached by the minister. His desire to leave the church where he had been baptized and raised, resulted in Milne receiving opposition from his relatives, especially from his mother and his sisters. Milne stayed for two years and then moved to George Cowie's Congregational church in Huntly, where he became a member a year after attending the church.[20]

Getting Ready: Calling, Training, Sending, and Going

George Cowie, born at Shank of Barry (ten miles from Banff, Aberdeenshire), was educated "for the ministry of the Anti-burgher section of the Secession Church, at Aberdeen University, . . . under Prof. [William] Moncrieff [c. 1729–1786], at the Alloa Theological Hall."[21] Being ordained on February 13, 1771, Cowie was the minister of five different parishes: Cabrach, Grange, Huntly, Keith, and Auchendion.[22] In 1775, Cowie found successors for the other four churches and only ministered at Huntly. At Huntly, Cowie was concerned not only about the congregation's spirituality (through evangelical preaching and Sunday evening schools), but also about

---

20. The Congregational church was founded by George Cowie in 1802, as a result of Cowie's controversy with the Presbytery and his dismissal in 1800. Though Cowie "acknowledged to his presbytery that he had acted wrongly in listening to the preaching of a minister of the Relief Church in 1782, he still persisted in cooperating with others in missionary societies and supported" James Haldane's (1768–1851) Independent teachings (Campbell, "Cowie, George," 1:261). The church building is located at Old Road and Stewart Lane, Huntly, Aberdeenshire. The church was closed in 1963, and now is a bakery factory.

21. W. B. R. W., "Notable Men & Women," 122. Anti-burgher, or Antiburgher, is "a member of the group in the Secession Church in Scotland which separated in 1747 from the 'Burgher' group because it refused to admit that an adherent of that Church could take the civil 'Burgess Oath.'" Cross and Lingstone, "Antiburgher," 77.

22. Mackelvie, *Annals and Statistics*, 90–91. These five locations are a few miles distance from each other, and Cowie continued this kind of ministry for four years.

Training Laborers for His Harvest

training men to become missionaries.[23] Therefore, Cowie's church was called "the Missionary *laigh* Kirk."[24]

As William Milne was born again in this "very cradle of Missions," Milne developed a special interest in missions, which earned him his first nickname, "*misshinir*."[25] Milne's missionary interest was deepened as he read Jonathan Edwards' (1703-1758) missionary biography of David Brainerd and the stories of missionaries that were published in magazines like the *Evangelical Magazine*. Milne later explained his missionary calling in his ordination service and stated that when he read the missionary stories, he "felt deeply concerned for the coming of Christ's kingdom among the nations."[26] With many prayers for the confirmation of his missionary calling, and his consultation with Christian friends, Milne sent in his application a second time to the London Missionary Society (LMS) through the Aberdeen Missionary Committee in about 1809.[27] While waiting for the committee's response, Milne devoted himself to prayer and reading books like the LMS' *Transactions of the Missionary Society*, Andrew Fuller's *Life of the Rev. Samuel Pearce*, and an articled entitled "To Pious Young Men" in *The Evangelical Magazine* (April 1805).[28] A month later, the Ab-

---

23. Anonymous, "Memoir of the Late Rev.," 124-25.

24. Philip, *Life and Opinion*, 28.

25. Ibid., 29.

26. Ibid., 33.

27. As early as 1805, Milne had first applied to the LMS, but was rejected. In April 1807, in a recommendation letter to John Philip (then at Aberdeen), Donald Morrison (1769-1846) a graduate of Hoxton Academy and an Independent minister of Huntly, wrote: "We have a young man, a member of our church, William Milne, aged 23 years, who has had for some time a great desire to offer himself to the Missionary Society. He has genuine piety, clear views of the doctrines of the Gospel, and good natural talents; and ardent desire for the glory of God, and the salvation of his fellow men. He wishes me to write to the directors concerning him; I hope as you will have an opportunity of seeing them, you will bring his case before them. If more information is necessary, I shall be ready to give it." Ellis, *The History*, 1:473.

28. See Morrison, *Memoirs*, 14; Philip, *Life and Opinion*, 36. Though in the text, the spelling is "Samuel Pierce," it is a spelling mistake of "Samuel Pearce," (1766-1799) Baptist minister of Cannon Street Baptist Church, Birmingham.

The Making of China's First Evangelist

erdeen committee called Milne for an interview; there, the committee suggested Milne should rather become a mechanic than a missionary.[29] Milne answered with a strong conviction of his confirmed missionary calling: "Anything, anything,—if only engaged in the work. I am willing to be a hewer of wood, or a drawer of water, in the Temple of my God."[30] The committee, being moved by Milne's servant-heart, accepted Milne's application and supported his travel to London, and then to Gosport, where he would receive missionary training from David Bogue (1750–1825).

Gosport Academy was opened by David Bogue at his home in Gosport, Hampshire in 1777. In 1800 Gosport Academy was affiliated with the LMS, becoming the LMS' official missionary training center. Bogue proposed a three-year curriculum for all missionary candidates trained in theological subjects, along with both scientific and humanistic subjects.[31] From 1809 to 1812, Milne trained under Bogue, which Milne later claimed was "one of the greatest blessings of his life . . . to have been under [Bogue's] care."[32] At Gosport, while devoted whole-heartedly to study, Milne never forget his church back in Huntly, and he requested Bogue "to leave him a whole hour every day for prayer on behalf of dear Huntly."[33] Milne's frequent correspondence with George Cowie, described the conditions of his studies at Gosport, requesting prayers as well as asking about the church's situation at Huntly. In a letter to Cowie, Milne wrote:

> I find the truth of what you warned me of,—that it is very difficult to maintain a lively sense and impression of

---

See Appendix 2: To Pious Young Men.

29. Philip, *Life and Opinion*, 43; Hancock, *Robert Morrison*, 92.
30. Philip, *Life and Opinion*, 43.
31. Originally, in order to save money, the LMS proposed a two-year program, but this proposal was disregarded by Bogue, based on his understanding of the qualification of a missionary. For a detailed study on Bogue's training vision and missionary strategy see Daily, "From Gosport to Canton," 95–136; Terpstra, "David Bogue"; Gibbard, "David Bogue," 36–41.
32. Philip, *Life and Opinion*, 48.
33. Ibid.

Training Laborers for His Harvest

the TRUTH on my heart, in the midst of study. I found a remark of Dr. Owen's [John Owen (1616–1683)] very true, that a person may be often speaking of religion, and yet have a very barren soul. . . . I find by experience, that it is not change of place nor employment that increases a Christian's spirituality of mind; but fresh, and confirming, and sanctifying discoveries of the greatness and glory of the Truth. How are matters at Huntly? We preach; but I am ready to think, that most of us would be but light metal amongst the good people at Huntly and Lesslie. . . O, that the Lord of the harvest may thrust forth right men! Would not James Skinner be persuaded?[34]

Robert Philip later comments, that from this letter, Milne's "judicious, discerning, and highly devotional" character was revealed.[35]

On July 16, 1812, after three years of missionary training, Milne was ordained at John Griffin's (1769–1834) church at Portsea, Portsmouth. At the service, John Hunt of Chelmsford, one of the directors of the LMS, offered opening prayer and Scripture reading. David Bogue made the introductory discourse. John Griffin asked four questions concerning Milne's conversion, missionary calling, missionary strategy, and theology. After answering these questions, Bogue offered an ordination prayer, which was followed by a sermon preached by James Bennet (1774–1862) from Jer 49:14, entitled, "An Ambassador is Sent to the Heathen." William Scamp (1774–1860) concluded the service with a prayer.[36]

Less than a month after his ordination, William Milne married Rachel Cowie (1783–1819) on August 4, 1812, at St. Leonard's, Shoreditch. The officiating officer was the curate Robert Crosby (1769–1837).[37] William and Rachel did not fall in love at first sight.

---

34. Ibid., 58–59.

35. Philip, *Life and Opinion*, 59.

36. The entire ordination service was recorded and published under the title, *The Ordination Services of the Rev[erend] William Milne and the Rev. George Thom; Missionaries to the East 1812*. Morrison, in his memoir, only kept the questions and answers on Milne's account. Morrison, *Memoirs*, 1–28.

37. According to the church's marriage register, this marriage was

The Making of China's First Evangelist

Though Rachel had heard a lot of good opinions about Milne from both Robert Philip and John Philip (1775–1851), neither Rachel (due to her humility) nor William (due to his focus on missionary preparation) ever thought of marrying each other. As Robert Philip put it, "they met and parted, without the shadow of an idea that they would ever meet again."[38] Robert Philip also recalled that, before Milne sailed to Gosport to study, Rachel "made him a present of some neckcloths."[39] Later, after Milne completed his studies at Gosport, he saw Rachel shared his missionary spirit—"her heart was too much affected with the wants of China"—and he saw her charming and joyful heart. He thus proposed and married her.[40] The marriage of William and Rachel impacted those on their mission field, especially Liang Fa (1789–1855), who would be baptized (1818) and mentored under the Milnes.[41]

A month later, on September 4, 1812, William and Rachel Milne sailed from Portsmouth for the Cape of Good Hope (today's Cape Town, South Africa). The Milnes arrived at the Cape of Good Hope on December 1, 1812. While at the Cape, the Milnes met some old friends and were introduced to John Herbert Harrington, Esq. (d. 1828), from whom Milne was able to collect information about Madagascar for both the LMS and Robert Morrison.[42] They also met another Scottish missionary, John Campbell (1766–1840), sent by the LMS. As the Milnes continued their voy-

---

performed under three witnesses. One is a George Smith, who was a widower, and married Martha Elsden on the same day right after William and Rachel Milne. The other two were John Cowie, who was Rachel's cousin, and lived in Hoxton; and Elizabeth Pates, who was "one of the sisters-in-law of Mr. Cowie, of Huntly [possibly George Cowie]," and lived in Ilford, Essex. See, Philip, *Life and Opinion*, 83–84. Marriage Register record see, *Guildhall, St. Leonard Shoreditch, Register of Marriages, Oct 1810–Dec 1812*, P91/LEN/A/01/ Ms7498/26. More biographical accounts of Rachel Cowie Milne, see Appendix 3: Memoir of Mrs. Milne.

38. Philip, *Life and Opinion*, 46.
39. Ibid.
40. Ibid., 82.
41. The Milnes' influence upon Liang Fa see, McNeur, *China's First Preacher*, 31–38.
42. Milne, *Retrospect*, 103.

25

age to China their missionary heart became stronger and more solidified. While at sea, William Milne kept himself busy, not only studying Scripture and the Chinese language, but also evangelizing and ministering to the sailors and fellow passengers, by leading worship and Bible study regularly.[43]

While William and Rachel Milne were still on their way to Macao, Robert and Mary Morton Morrison were patiently waiting for what they had prayed and requested for many years. On July 4, 1813, William and Rachel Milne arrived at Macao and were "most cordially welcomed by" the Morrisons.[44] On that night, Morrison prayed, expressing his deep longings, "Thus far (blessed be the great Disposer of events) the door has been opened. O that the Lord's servant [referring to Milne] may be spared in health, may soon acquire the language of the heathen, and be a faithful missionary of Jesus Christ."[45]

Bringing the Gospel to the Chinese at Malacca

Early in the morning on July 9, 1813, a sergeant from the Portuguese Governor, Bernardo Aleixo de Lemos e Faria (1754–1826), came to Morrison with a verbal command that Milne "must leave in eight days."[46] Though Morrison was friendly to the Governor, "the Governor's position was clear, and 'unanswerable.'"[47] The Governor's coldness to Morrison was not personal; rather he was under the influence of the Roman Catholic bishop and clergy, "who were alarmed at the arrival of a Protestant missionary, to whom they could show no indulgence, notwithstanding, at the same time

---

43. Milne also drew "Rules for Ship-Master," for the captain during this time. Philip, *Life and Opinion*, 95–99.

44. Milne, *Retrospect*, 103.

45. Morrison, *Memoirs*, 1:365.

46. Ibid.

47. Hancock, *Robert Morrison*, 94. According to Morrison, under his negotiation the Governor would "extend the eight days to eighteen," is different than Edwin Stevens' account that Milne had to leave in "24 hours." Morrison, *Memoirs*, 1:366; Stevens, "A Brief Sketch," 319.

The Making of China's First Evangelist

a great number of their own body were hospitably entertained, and even kindly fostered in the heart of England."[48] Meanwhile, Morrison asked if the East India Company (EIC) would hire Milne, which had hired Morrison, but the EIC refused to hire Milne permanently. What the EIC offered was to hire Milne as an assistant to Morrison for only eight months to help Morrison to complete the English-Chinese dictionary. Morrison was disappointed by the EIC, since he felt "betrayed by friends in the English community."[49] Morrison then sent Milne to Canton for the winter. On July 20, leaving a pregnant Rachel with Mary Morrison at Macao, Milne "went in a small boat to Canton, where [he] remained the ensuing season; enjoying that hospitality among the heathen, which had been denied in a Christian colony."[50] Christopher Hancock concludes that this event "set them [Morrison and Milne] in good stead for the future," as Milne would become "a close friend," "intellectual peer," and "constant help" to Morrison.[51]

Life for Milne in Canton was not easy since Milne had to hide himself in a factory at the port, which cost him expansively "500 Spanish dollars for the season," as the Chinese government was very cautious about foreigners.[52] While he was in Canton, Milne followed Morrison's three core principles in learning Chinese:

---

48. Anonymous, "Memoir of the Late Rev.," 137–38.

49. Hancock, *Robert Morrison*, 95.

50. On October 14, 1813, Rachel delivered their first child, a daughter, named Amelia. At this time, William was able to have a brief trip back to Macao to visit his Rachel and Amelia. Amelia was not baptized until January 23, 1814. Milne, *Retrospect*, 105, 107.

51. Hancock, *Robert Morrison*, 96, 93.

52. Milne, *Retrospect*, 107. William Milne described Canton as "like the New Jerusalem only in one thing; that *strangers* are not permitted to enter. I have once peeped in at the gate; and I hope yet to enter. A few days ago, I went to the top of a little hill to view this land, . . . My thoughts were 'O that God would give this land to the churches, that we, their Messengers, might walk through the length and breadth of it, to publish the glory of His salvation! . . . I think them [Chinese] exceedingly corrupted in their morals. They are a civilized and industrious people; but their land is *full* of idols!" Philip, *Life and Opinion*, 111.

Training Laborers for His Harvest

1. to learn the colloquial dialect first, to enable questions and conversation;
2. to commit much to memory. The practice of the Chinese themselves . . .
3. to pay attention to characters: "a few characters should every day be written and carefully analyzed."[53]

It was certainly difficult for Milne to learn Chinese in such a difficult situation. Within six months, Milne's Chinese had improved dramatically, yet Milne still described the language study as "a work for men with bodies of brass, lungs of steel, heads of oak, hands of spring-steel, eyes of eagles, hearts of apostles, memories of angels, and lives of Methuselah! Still I make a little progress."[54]

Early in 1814, Milne took Morrison's suggestion to take a seven-month missionary journey to the islands in the South Sea, such as Java, Batavia, and Malacca where he would distribute the Chinese New Testament and tracts among the Chinese.[55] After the trip, Milne returned to Canton in the winter, opening his rooms to foreign residents and seamen to attend public worship.

As early as September 1814, both the Portuguese colonial government and Chinese government made resolutions to the disadvantage of Protestant missionaries.[56] Seeing the negative

---

53. Hancock, *Robert Morrison*, 106.

54. Philip, *Life and Opinion*, 137.

55. Milne, *Retrospect*, 114–20; Hancock, *Robert Morrison*, 100–03. The year 1814 was special for both Morrison and Milne, since on July 16, 1814, Morrison baptized their first convert, Tsae A-ko (1788–1818), who was first introduced to Morrison by Yong Sam-tak to be employed Morrison's printer. Su Ching comments, "since the convert was the first reaped by the Protestant mission on Chinese soil, his conversion may certainly be seen as an event of historical significance." Su, "First Protestant Convert of China," 227–28. Detailed studies on Tsae A-ko see, Su, "First Protestant Convert of China," 227–43; Chang, "Chung-Hua Ti-I-Tz'u Shou-His-Jen," 154–56.

56. The Roman Catholic clergy at Macao complained about Morrison and Milne's activities and about the tracts they handed to the Portuguese. On the other hand, the Chinese government ordered "no natives to serve foreigners, but winks at it. The practice goes on till the government wishes to annoy and dismiss the resident foreigners, when the law is then enforced." Morrison,

The Making of China's First Evangelist

change of their missionary situation, both Morrison and Milne agreed to establish a missionary station outside of Macao and Canton, where Protestants would be welcomed both by the officials and within Chinese settlements. They found Malacca to be the best place for such a station, since at the time Malacca was a British colony, governed by the friendly Scottish-born Major-General William Farquhar (1774-1839). On April 17, 1815, William and the again-pregnant Rachel Milne sailed to Malacca with their young daughter Amelia. Liang Fa also went with the Milnes as a printer. On April 22, Rachel gave birth to twin boys at sea, named William Charles and Robert George.[57] The Milne household arrived at Malacca, on the Malay Peninsula, on May 21, 1815, and was once again warmly welcomed by Farquhar.

Soon after the Milnes arrived and settled at Malacca, Morrison laid out some significant principles in a letter on July 15, 1815, for Milne's mission at Malacca. First, "their vision is to expand the scope of the Mission in keeping with the 'conversion of the Chinese, and of all who speak their language.'"[58] For Morrison and Milne, they understood that their primary missionary task

---

Memoirs, 1:410. Some scholars, like Jean-Pierre Charbonnier, recently argue that the Roman Catholic clergy were peaceful towards the Protestant missionaries, and say that it was the Protestants who refused to cooperate with them. This is contrary to the facts at Macao, since Morrison and Milne thought the Catholics were "peaceable people," and it was the Catholic clergy who complained about jealousy. Compare Charbonnier, *Christians in China*, 350-64; with Milne, *Retrospect*, 128, and Peyrefitte, *Immobile Empire*, xxiii-xxiv.

57. William Charles Milne (April 22, 1815-May 16, 1863) was ordained on July 19, 1837, and appointed by the LMS to Canton as a missionary. William Charles later became assistant Chinese secretary to the legation at Beijing. He married Frances-Williamina, daughter of Rev. Dr. Joseph Beaumont (1794-1855), on August 27, 1846. William Charles died on May 15, 1863 of apoplexy, and he was buried at the Russian cemetery, outside of the North gate of Beijing. Robert George Milne (April 22, 1815-November 20, 1882), studied and graduated from Marischal College, Aberdeen University with his twin brother William Charles. Robert George married Catherine Bradley (1816-1860). On April 14, 1841, Robert George was ordained in Providence Chapel, Whitehaven, Cumberland, and became a Congregationalist minister first at Tintwistle, Chester, and later at Southport, Lancaster.

58. Hancock, *Robert Morrison*, 113.

was to reach the Chinese, and they were not to be sidetracked by establishing a station outside of China. Second, "their vision is to establish a headquarters for the work," which they want to be "a head-quarters at which to meet and consult, from which to commission persons to go forth on every hand,--a home to which to retire in case of sickness or declining years."[59] In other words, the station at Malacca was a temporary harbor from the persecutions. Third, "their vision [was] to set up a school 'for the instruction of Native and European youth; for the reception and initiation of young missionaries from Europe.'"[60] The Anglo-Chinese College opened in 1818.

According to these three principles, Milne took charge of the missionary station at Malacca. So Su summarized the various works for which Milne busied himself at Malacca:[61]

1. Purchase land and establish mission houses;
2. Oral labors—preaching and teaching;[62]
3. Education, specifically being the principal of the Anglo-Chinese College;
4. Printing;[63]

59. Ibid.
60. Ibid.
61. Su, *Open Up, China!*, 144–68.
62. A schedule of Milne's oral labors is recorded in both Morrison's *Memoir* and Milne's *Retrospect*. Milne would preach in three languages, English, Chinese, and Malay. On regular Sundays: preach in Chinese at 7 am; in English at 10 am (as the minister of Dutch Reformed Church, Malacca); catechizing in Chinese at 12 pm; catechizing in English at 7 pm; and catechizing in Malay at 8:30 pm. On weekdays, Milne would have a 10 to 15 minute worship service at the mission house. Every morning or afternoon, Milne would teach his children. Every Tuesday night, Milne would have a prayer meeting with Liang Fa. Every Wednesday and Friday night, Milne would teach A-Kang and Meen-Ko. Every Monday, Wednesday and Friday at 4 pm, Milne would read the Scripture with Liang Fa. Every Thursday afternoon around five, Milne would catechize one or two youth in English, and that night around eight, Milne would preach at Ta-Peh-Kung Temple to around fifty people in Chinese. Every Saturday or Wednesday afternoon, Milne would catechize women. Morrison, *Memoir*, 89–90; Milne, *Retrospect*, 144–45.

63. Milne's major contribution to the printed media are, (1) the first

The Making of China's First Evangelist

5. Writing and editing;[64]
6. Establishing the Ultra-Ganges Mission in 1818.

In addition to these six labors, Milne also devoted time to mentoring his printer Liang Fa, leading him from a heathen to a believer, and from a believer to a solid Gospel apologist and evangelist.

"BEFORE I CAME HITHER, I KNEW NOT GOD; NOW I DESIRE TO SERVE HIM."[65]

Liang Fa, or Leang Kung-Fa, was born in 1789, in Gulao village, Sanzhou (three islands) town, Gaoming (lofty clearness) county, Zhaoqing Fu (肇慶府高明縣三洲古勞村), about seventy miles from Canton, in Guangdong province.[66] Like Morrison and Milne, Liang's "origins were humble but his achievements remarkable."[67] Liang's parents were poor, yet they sent him to a village school at the age of eleven. During his four years of school, Liang "committed to memory the Four Books, the Five Classics, and the Sacred Edict, [which] the two former sets bring the ancient Confucian classics and the last a series of moral maxims written by the second emperor of" Qing dynasty.[68] In 1804, Liang left his village for Canton where he "found work with a maker of Chinese brush pens,

---

Chinese Bible, translated by Morrison and Milne; (2) Gospel tracts; (3) the first Chinese magazine, *Chinese Monthly Magazine* 察世俗每月統記傳 (August 5,1815– January1821); (4) English magazine, *Indo-Chinese Gleaner* (1815–1822); (5) and other publications, including Milne's *Retrospect*.

64. During his seven-year ministry at Malacca, Milne wrote seventeen tracts, among which "Dialogues Between Chang and Yuan 張遠兩友相論" (1819) was the most influential. It was revised and well-read in China until 1949. Milne also translated David Bogue's commentary on Ephesians, and several Chinese classics in English. Until his death, Milne was the chief editor of the English magazine *Indo-Chinese Gleaner*.

65. Philip, *Life and Opinion*, 225–26.

66. Li, *History of Early Christian Missionary in China*, 175, n. 17; McNeur, *China's First Preacher*, 7.

67. Hancock, *Robert Morrison*, 93.

68. McNeur, *China's First Preacher*, 11–12.

but very soon left this occupation and apprenticed himself to an engraver of wooden printing blocks."⁶⁹ In 1810, Liang was called home on account of the death of his mother and soon returned to Canton and was employed at a printing house around the Thirteen Factories. In September, Morrison was looking to publish his translation of the book of Acts, and Liang was hired to carve its wooden printing blocks. It is because of Liang's steadiness and excellent skills in carving that he soon gained Morrison's trust and continued being employed in Morrison's Chinese translation of the New Testament during 1811 and 1812.⁷⁰

In April 1815, when Milne sailed to Malacca, Liang was with him, "to assist in printing Chinese books."⁷¹ Shortly after arriving in Malacca, Liang "fell into deep despair over his years of gambling and intemperance in Canton," and Liang "saw his anxiety in spiritual terms."⁷² In a sense, like his mentor Milne, Liang was raised in a religious culture. Though he had participated in Buddhist Pure Land rites, which are commonly practiced by the Chinese focusing on Amitābha Buddha, Liang had later "regarded religious matters with careless indifference."⁷³ For Liang, at Malacca, there were many uncertainties, as to whether to stay far away from home and whom he would marry. According to Chinese traditions, Liang went to the local temple of the Overseas Chinese community in Malacca on the first and fifteenth day of every month to burn incense and "to implore Kuan-yin's compassionate intercessions for protection, blessing, and eventual entrance into Amitābha's Western Paradise."⁷⁴ One conversation with a Chinese Buddhist monk made Liang start to detest Buddhism, as the monk advised him to "accumulate sufficient merit to outweigh his misdeeds," which is obtained through "joining the sangha (by which he could remit the sins of himself and his entire family), donating money for temple

69. Ibid., 14.
70. Li, *History of Early Christian Missionary in China*, 175, n. 17.
71. Wylie, *Memorials*, 21.
72. Bohr, "Liang Fa's *Quest*," 37.
73. Ibid.
74. Ibid., 37–38.

The Making of China's First Evangelist

repair . . . and the daily recitation of sutras."[75] For Liang, the monk was carrying a business, rather than helping him to save his soul.

Meanwhile, William Milne had finished his 71-page tract, "Life of Christ" (求世者言行真史記) which was a booklet that "notices the creation, providence, sin and misery of man."[76] Liang was hired to carve the blocks for printing this tract. Later, before Liang's baptism, he told Milne that, while he was laboring on the carving, the text brought to him some new ideas about Christianity.[77] Liang then began to read Morrison's New Testament, attend Milne's preaching, and seek Milne's help on certain difficult biblical passages. P. Richard Bohr states that "Christianity's greatest attraction for him [Liang] was the notion of filiality and moral seriousness emerging from the concept of monotheism."[78]

In the summer of 1816, Milne wrote in his journal that Liang "professed his determination to take up his cross and follow Christ."[79] After private conversations, testing his faith and prayers, William Milne baptized Liang Fa on November 3, 1816. Milne recorded in his journal that "the service was performed privately, in a room of the Mission-house. Care had been taken, by "private conversation, instruction, and prayer, to prepare him for this sacred ordination."[80] Milne found clear spiritual change in Liang's life as "he was formerly stiff and obstinate, and occasionally troublesome," but now "there has been scarcely any thing of this kind to complain of."[81] As Milne found no reasons to delay baptism, he posed five questions to Liang at his baptism:

> *Question 1.* Have you truly turned from idols, to worship and serve the living and true God, the creator of heaven and earth, and all things?

---

75. Ibid., 38.
76. Wylie, *Memorials*, 14.
77. Philip, *Life and Opinion*, 225.
78. Bohr, "Liang Fa's *Quest for Moral Power*," 39.
79. Philip, *Life and Opinion*, 224.
80. Ibid.
81. Ibid., 225.

Answer. This is my heart's desire.

Q. 2. Do you know and feel that you are a sinful creature, totally unable to save yourself?

A. I know it.

Q. 3. Do you really, from your heart, believe that Jesus Christ is the Son of God, and Saviour of the world; and do you trust in him alone for salvation?

A. This is my heart's desire.

Q. 4. Do you expect any worldly advantage, profit, or gain whatever, by your becoming a Christian?

A. None: I receive baptism because it is my duty.

Q. 5. Do you resolve from this day till the day of your death, to live in obedience to all the commandments and ordinances of God; and in justice and righteousness of life before him?

A. This is my determination; but I fear my strength is not equal to it.[82]

Milne further wrote, "since his [Liang's] baptism, some private means have been used to increase his knowledge; to impress his heart more deeply, and to strengthen his faith."[83] Milne began his mentorship and theological education with Liang. Under Milne's supervision and editing, Liang wrote a 37-page tract, "Miscellaneous Exhortations (救世錄撮要略解)," which contains "a preface concerning God as the Creator, and object of worship, to which the Ten Commandments are attached," along with some New Testament passages, and "three hymns and prayers."[84] Under Morrison's approval, two hundred copies of Liang's tract were printed so that he could distribute them to his relatives and neighbors.

In 1819, Liang went back to his home village, and married a woman whose family name was Lai.[85] While at home, this

---

82. Ibid., 226–27; also see McNeur, *China's First Preacher*, 28–29.
83. Philip, *Life and Opinion*, 227.
84. Wylie, *Memorials*, 22.
85. In imperial China, a married woman, either a wife or a concubine,

The Making of China's First Evangelist

"new-born" Liang was burdened with his friends' sin, especially their idolatry, and decided to share his tract with them. Possibly some printers secretly reported him to the police, and both his tracts and blocks were destroyed, and Liang was put in prison. As soon as Morrison received this news, he tried to ask the Thirteen Factory traders to help obtain Liang's release, and as a result, Liang received "thirty blows with the bamboo, and had seventy dollars extorted from him," with the charge of having been overseas.[86] Liang was then released. Later, after Liang's release, his wife was converted and baptized by him.

In the spring of 1820, Liang went back to Malacca to study and work with Milne, until Milne's death in 1822. On November 20, 1823, Liang's son was baptized by Morrison, and named Liang Jinde (梁進德 [1820–1862]). Liang now was employed by the LMS as a native teacher. In 1827, Liang was ordained by Morrison as China's first evangelist. For many years, Liang "continued zealously to compose print and distribute Christian books among his countrymen in the province of Guangdong, frequently attending at the literary examinations for that purpose, as well in the district cities as in the provincial capital."[87] Though Milne was not able to witness Liang's contribution to the early Protestant mission in China, especially in places where Morrison and Milne were not able to visit and stay, God listened to Milne's prayer, as he hoped Liang would "be faithful unto death; and as he is the first fruits of this branch of the Mission, may an abundant harvest follow, to the joy of the church, and the honour of Christ."[88] On April 12, 1855, Liang died at home at the age of sixty-seven. By this time, due to the labor of Morrison, Milne, and other missionaries who had labored, the seed of the Gospel was deeply planted in China.

---

would be referred to "by her husband's last name, followed by her father's last name, and then the honorific *shi* [which means "born as"]." Bernhardt, *Women and Property in China*, 27, n. 9. On Chinese names see Hucker, *China's Imperial Past*, 438–39.

86. Wylie, *Memorials*, 22.
87. Wylie, *Memorials*, 21–22.
88. Philip, *Life and Opinion*, 227.

For Liang Fa, he also left a pious legacy to both the Chinese church and his family.[89]

THE BITTERNESS OF DEPARTURE

With deep conviction, the Milnes left their comfortable homeland, and for the sake of lost souls in China, they endured various trials and hardship. After William and Rachel's wedding, Robert Philip wrote of their friends at the wedding, "there we parted to meet no more on earth; but pledged to meet often in spirit at the Throne of Grace."[90] The Milnes never returned to Scotland. They died and were buried at Malacca, the place where they settled and labored.

Shortly after Rachel gave birth to the twin boys, she conceived again, and gave birth to David in 1816 and Sarah in 1817. Both David and Sarah died within a week of their birth, and this loss affected Rachel greatly. Two years after Sarah's death, on February 6, 1819, Rachel gave birth to their youngest son, and William named him after his friend General Farquhar. After the delivery, Rachel became seriously ill, and she was not able to get out of her bed. As a result, Farquhar was baptized at the side of Rachel's deathbed at nine o'clock on the night of February 5, 1819.

As Rachel noticed that her days were drawing nigh, she started to ask William to pray, read Scripture and hymns to her, that her soul might be in peace from her physical suffering.[91] Rachel died on March 20, 1819. Her funeral was held at eight o'clock in the morning the next day, with friends singing Rachel's favorite hymn, "God Moves in a Mysterious Way," which was written by William Cowper. In a letter to Morrison, Milne wrote, "My Rachel's dying under my own care, where I saw the worst, and performed the last duties with my own hands, has been a source of satisfaction to me."[92]

---

89. McNeur, *China's First Preacher*, 117–23.
90. Philip, *Life and Opinion*, 84.
91. Ibid., 291–303.
92. Ibid., 329.

The Making of China's First Evangelist

On November 26, 1820, due to Milne's contribution to the Chinese Bible translation, and his work at Malacca, William Taylor (1744–1823), the principal of the University of Glasgow, bestowed on Milne an honorary degree of Doctor of Divinity (D.D.). Milne became the second person of the Ultra-Ganges Mission to receive a D.D., since Robert Morrison had received a D.D. from the same university on December 24, 1817.[93]

For Morrison, he treasured his friendship and partnership with Milne, since "Milne had the creativity, freedom, and personality Morrison lacked," so when Milne's time of departure came in 1822, it was a great loss to Morrison.[94] After Rachel's death, William Milne's burden had been doubled, since he was already very busy with his mission work, and now he also had to take care of his children and daily family duties. Such pressure and heavy load of work consumed William's health, and made him sick towards the end of 1821. From May 24, 1822, Milne's body became weaker and weaker. Though "during his last illness he seldom spoke," Milne expressed his wish, that "if his illness should end in death, that his body should be opened." On June 2, 1822, Milne died, and as his body was opened. His colleague found his lungs, "on the right side, adhered to the ribs; they had lost their natural colour, and were covered with small swellings."[95] At four o'clock the same day, Milne's body was carried from the Anglo-Chinese College to the Dutch cemetery of "St. Anthony on the side of St. Paul's Hill."[96] Milne was buried with his Rachel and two pre-deceased children, David and Sarah.[97] The funeral was held at the Dutch Reformed

---

93. Ibid., 288; Hancock, *Robert Morrison*, 136–41.
94. Ibid., 134.
95. Philip, *Life and Opinion*, 110–111.
96. Harrison, *Waiting for China*, 66.
97. After the death of Rachel and William Milne, their daughter Amelia, and sons William Charles, Robert George and Farquhar were sent back to England. With the help of Andrew Reed (1785–1862) of Wycliff Chapel, Milne's children were funded for education, and found a home in their relatives. In an 1832 article of *Chinese Repository*, it was said that Amelia, the eldest child of Milne, was "expected soon to accompany a lady of great respectability to Malacca, for the purpose of giving to Pagan and Mohammedan girls a Christian

Training Laborers for His Harvest

Church with numerous attendees, and "there were also hundreds of natives, both Chinese and Malay, as spectators."[98]

Milne died, yet the gospel did not die in China. As Morrison wrote about Milne's death:

> Hume, who essayed to subvert the cause of God and of Christ on earth, died jesting; and Milne, who labored to promote the cause of Christ and of God, died mourning. Shall the manner of a man's death then, be considered as a proof or disproof of the justice and goodness of his cause![99]

For William and Rachel Milne, the bud of laboring in China and Malacca may have been bitter, yet God rooted their ministry and caused it to bloom into the sweet flower of the gospel in China!

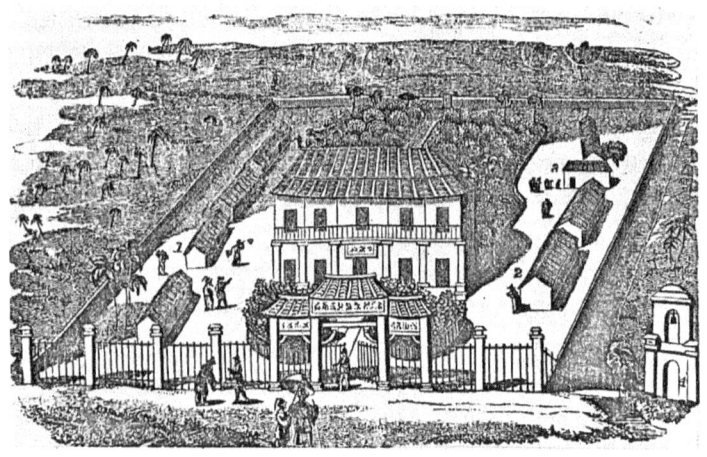

1. Chinese Printing Office   2. English Printing Office   3. Chinese School   4. Western Gate of Malacca

Figure 4: The Anglo-Chinese College

---

education" (Stevens, "Brief Sketch," 325). In Andrew Reed's memoirs, it was said that Amelia was a member of Reed's Wycliff Chapel at New Road, London, and "after a short life of lovely promise, died in the midst of her usefulness." (Reed and Reed, *Memoirs*, 263) William, Robert and Farquhar would later sent to Marischal College under the care of a James Milne (Royal Commissioners, *Second Report*, 139).

98. Philip, *Life and Opinion*, 111.
99. Morrison, *Memoirs*, 112.

3

The Theology of William Milne

> Q. What is the chief end of man?
> A. Man's chief end is to glorify God, and to enjoy him for ever.
>
> Westminster Shorter Catechism

> Q. What way should you serve God?
> A. By obeying his commands and trusting in him, by reading, hearing, prayer, and praise.
>
> The Mother's Catechism

WITH THE COMPLETION OF the biographical sketches of both William Milne and Liang Fa, we arrive at this chapter, which aims to explore and analyze Milne's theology in context. This chapter will prepare us for the detailed studies on Milne's mentorship of Liang in the next chapter.

According to Milne's account of himself at his ordination service, there were three major periods in his theological formation: prior to conversion, discipleship after conversion, and formal theological education.¹ However, given his pioneer role in translating the Scripture and composing evangelical tracts in Chinese, Milne's theology was also sharpened by his linguistic and cultural studies in China.²

BEFORE CONVERSION: SCOTTISH PRESBYTERIANISM

After the death of Oliver Cromwell (1599–1658), the exiled Charles II (1630–1685) was welcomed back by the Royalist-dominated parliament in May 1660. The English monarchy was thus restored. Under Charles' influence, the Convention Parliament passed a series of acts on religious conformity, which became known as the "Clarendon Code." With the "Great Ejection" taking place in 1662, nonconformist church meetings became illegal.³ Puritans lost their political momentum in England.

Following in the steps of his grandfather James I (1566–1625) and his father Charles I (1600–1649), Charles II reinstated episcopacy in Scotland, and sought to converge the Scottish and English national churches.⁴ This was strongly opposed by the Presbyterian Covenanters, and they were brutally suppressed by the state in the 1680s. This was the religious persecution recorded in *The Cloud of Witnesses*, of which Milne read before his conversion. Following the Glorious Revolution of 1688, with the major allegiance to Presbyterianism by the Scottish, and under the toleration of William III (1650–1702), Presbyterianism was settled as Scotland's national church, and was further secured by the legislative union of 1707. For the Presbyterians, the Calvinistic

> *Westminster Confession* was . . . held to be subordinate to Scripture and to derive its authority from Scripture. But it was also held to be the perfect compend of Scripture

---

1. Morrison, *Memoirs*, 1–11.
2. Cf. Walls, *Missionary Movement*, 195–98.
3. See Thompson, "Great Ejection," 161–82.
4. Brown, "Religion in Scotland," 261.

The Theology of William Milne

doctrine, and therefore the perfect norm for the correct interpretation of Scripture, which the Church must uphold at all costs.[5]

Thus, the Church of Scotland was primarily Calvinistic. As paedobaptists, Scottish Presbyterians emphasized their children's religious education. In 1696, the Act for Settling of Schools was passed by the Scottish Parliament directing that schools should be provided in every parish and supervised by presbyteries. From an early age, children would be taught with Calvinistic doctrines using standard textbooks like *The Shorter Catechism* and the Bible.[6]

In the early eighteenth century, there were two theological controversies within the Scottish church, which were "over the alleged antinomianism and universalism of the teaching of *The Marrow of Modern Divinity* by Edward Fisher [fl. 1627–1655]," and over "the alleged rationalism and Socinianism of Professor John Simson of Glasgow."[7] Only the Marrow controversy will be examined here, as Thomas Boston was directly involved in it.

Originally published by Fisher in 1646 in England, *The Marrow* was in the genre of a dialogue between Evangelista (a minister of the Gospel), Nomista (a legalist), Antinomista (an Antinomian), and Neophitus (a young Christian), and dealt with "the relations of the law and grace under the Gospel, and laid strong emphasis on the part of grace in the saving of men."[8] With Boston's endorsements, *The Marrow* was reprinted in 1718 by James Hog (c. 1658–1734), minister of Carnock and friend of Boston. This concerned the General Assembly, first challenged by James Hadow (1667–1747), the principal of St. Mary's College, St. Andrews. Hadow, took a neonomian position and argued about "the Antinomian tendencies of [*The Marrow*], and tabulate passages in which its teaching deviated from that of the *Confession of Faith*."[9] In 1720,

---

5. Burleigh, *Church History of Scotland*, 287.

6. See Law, "Scottish Schoolbooks," 1–32.

7. Torrance, *Scottish Theology*, 223. On the Simson controversy see Torrance, *Scottish Theology*, 229–32; Burleigh, *Church History of Scotland*, 287–88.

8. Ibid., 288.

9. Ibid., 289.

The Marrow was condemned by the General Assembly, the majority supporting neonomianism. The next year, Boston annotated and published another edition of *The Marrow*, and defended it in his *Human Nature in Its Fourfold State*. In 1721, at the General Assembly, a group of twelve ministers submitted a *Representation and Petition*, refuting the condemnation of Antinomianism and Universalism.[10] Boston believed that "his distinction of free justification and resultant sanctification was the necessary alternative to Catholic and Arminian conflation of saving grace and human response."[11] In his response, Boston was clear in subscribing to the doctrine of particular redemption and penal substitution in the Confession, yet differentiated in assurance, which was not a subjective "kind of assurance . . . but an assurance which is in faith . . . a fiducial appropriating persuasion."[12] Nevertheless, the "Marrow men" also believed the absolute and unconditional free offer of the gospel, contrary to their opponents' language.[13] James Walker, thus, commented, "Boston and the Marrow men, first of all among our divines, entered fully into the missionary spirit of the Bible."[14]

In the eighteenth century, with the Scottish Enlightenment and the Great Awakening, Presbyterians in Scotland were divided as the Moderates and the Evangelicals. The Moderates were led by William Robertson (1721–1793), who worked to lead the church "away from the rough-hewn, militant religion . . . towards a more

---

10. These twelve "Marrow men" were Thomas Boston of Ettrick, James Hog of Carnock, John Bonar (1671–1747) of Torphichen, John Williamson (c. 1680–1740) of Inveresk, James Kid of Queensferry, Gabriel Wilson (1679–1750) of Maxton, Ebenezer Erskine (1680–1754) of Portmoak, Ralph Erskine (1685–1752) of Dunfermline, James Wardlaw of Dunfermline, Henry Davidson (1687–1756) of Galashiels, James Bathgate (d. 1727) of Orwell, and William Hunter (1657–1736) of Lilliesleaf.

11. Pastoor and Johnson, *A to Z of the Puritans*, 198.

12. Fisher and Boston, *Marrow of Modern Divinity*, 163.

13. Detailed studies on the theology of the "Marrow men" see VanDoodewaard, *Marrow Controversy*, 59–112; Lachman, *Marrow Controversy*; Makidon, "Marrow Controversy." On analysis of Boston's theology see McGowan, *Federal Theology of Thomas Boston*.

14. Walker, *Theology and Theologians*, 94.

The Theology of William Milne

cultivated, tolerant, world-affirming faith."[15] Rooted in "the spirit of inquiry and criticism that characterized the Enlightenment, and in the feeling for culture . . ." Moderatism soon dominated in the Church of Scotland.[16] Doctrinally, the Moderates were tepid orthodox, who emphasized more practical morality and general revelation in nature and human reason, than Calvinistic doctrines like predestination and total depravity.[17] Thus, the Moderates preached "cold morality" and "'legalism' without a touch of gospel to stir or comfort souls."[18]

As a part of the eighteenth-century transatlantic evangelical awakening, the Scottish evangelicals emphasized "individual conversion experience, regular Bible reading, participation in prayer meetings and an emotional, heartfelt piety."[19] This was reflected in the teachings of the "Marrow Men" and ministers like John Willison (1680–1750) of Dundee, John Erskine (1721–1803) and Thomas Chalmers (1780–1847).[20] In their preaching, the Evangelicals emphasized the individual's need of new birth, which was reflected in the rise of popular conversion narratives.[21] Along with evangelical preaching, the Evangelicals also emphasized "a more dogmatic approach to theology."[22]

Beside *The Shorter Catechism*, *The Cloud of Witnesses* and Boston, John Willison was another one who influenced Milne, mainly through Willison's *Mother's Catechism* and *A Sacramental Directory*.[23] Though Willison was one of the ministers who

15. Brown, "Religion in Scotland," 267.
16. Burleigh, *Church History of Scotland*, 295.
17. Brown, "Religion in Scotland," 267.
18. Burleigh, *Church History of Scotland*, 304; Clark, "From Protest to Reaction," 207–08.
19. Brown, "Religion in Scotland," 267.
20. See Fawcett, *Cambuslang Revival*; Schmidt, *Holy Fairs*; Roxborough, *Thomas Chalmers*.
21. On conversion narrative see Hindmarsh, *The Evangelical Conversion Narrative*, 1–87, 193–225.
22. McIntosh, *Church and Theology in Enlightenment Scotland*, 176.
23. Morrison, *Memoirs*, 2–3.

opposed the "Marrow men," David C. Lachman identified that Willison held a theological position "virtually identical with those of the Marrow Brethren."[24] Though older than Jonathan Edwards (1703–1758), Willison was an enthusiastic follower and promoter of Edwards' works, as he wrote prefaces for two of Edwards' works when they were republished in England, which were Edwards' treatise "Distinguished Marks of the Work of the Spirit of God" and his sermon "Sinners in the Hands of an Angry God."[25] Willison's evangelical spirit was also manifested in his *Mother's Catechism*, which was written in relatively simple language, and "nearer to a child's understand than *The Shorter Catechism*."[26] There are about four hundred questions and answers in the catechism, with "historical questions for children out of the Bible," "the Ten Commandments in metre," and morning and evening prayers.

In summary, according to Milne's personal account, even before his conversion, Milne was educated with Calvinistic doctrines. Though Milne grew up in a Moderate church, which probably oppose the "Marrow man," he was still able to learn from the evangelicals by reading Boston's *Fourfold State* and Willison's works.[27] Milne's reading of evangelical literature, along with his memory of the Westminster doctrines and Cowie's evangelical preaching, eventually led him to a heart-felt religion.

Milne's early religious education influenced him in his missionary field, not only reflected in his willingness to be martyred for his faith as his forefathers in *The Cloud of Witnesses*, but also in his continuous use of the method of catechesis to the Chinese. In 1817, Milne wrote and published a tract, which he named 幼學淺解問答 ("A Catechism for Youth") in Malacca. In this catechism, Milne posed 165 questions. Differing from *The Shorter Catechism* and

---

24. Lachman, *Marrow Controversy*, 198–99; also see Mitchell, "Jonathan Edwards's Scottish Connection," 77.

25. Mitchell, "Jonathan Edwards's Scottish Connection," 230.

26. Law, "Scottish Schoolbooks," 6.

27. In Milne's personal account, he commented on the preaching of his old parish church which was noted was "chiefly legal and moral." Morrison, *Memoirs*, 9.

Willison's *Mother's Catechism*, Milne began by asking why a youth should come to learn under a "fu shi" (父師, lit. "father-teacher").[28] The answer was to "receive the teachings of 'fu shi,'" in order to "know the true God, myself, humanity, and all my duties."[29] In question 4, Milne asked "Who is God?" and the answer was "the one who created the heaven, earth and all that is in them."[30] Questions 5 to 11 was about human beings in body and spirit, the difference between humans and animals, and why God created humans different from the rest of the creatures. In question 12, Milne asked, "How could you know, and serve God?" The answer was "I have to read the one Holy Bible respectively, since it proclaims God's truth. So by studying it, I would know the true God, and serve him."[31] Questions 13 and 14 were about the nature of the Bible. Questions 15 to 18 was about God's nature, the Trinity, and God's relationship with his creatures. Then, from questions 19 to 37, Milne expanded on men's duties, the Ten Commandments, how to love God, and how to love one other. Questions 38 to 41 were about humanity and human society. Questions 42 to 89 addressed the topic of sin, pardon of sin, total depravity, the meaning of the gospel, and doctrines relate to Christology and soteriology. Questions 90 to 113 then focused on the issues of the church, ministers, baptism and the Lord's Supper.

28. In Chinese, the normal usage of the phrase would be "師父" (lit., "teacher-father"), which means "master" in English, but Milne on purpose emphasized the master's paternal responsibility in catechizing his children. See Milne, *Catechism*, 6.

29. Ibid., 15.
一問，愛子弟，因何意而來此耶。(Q 1, Why have you come to me, my dear child?)
答曰，小子來此是受父師之教也。(Answer: To receive father-teacher's teaching is this boy's reason here)
二問，愛子弟，既有此意是甚好也，但教于你身果何益耶。(Q 2, My dear child, it is good for your wish, but what would be good for you to be taught?)
答曰，小子得教，纔可知道真神，知道自己，知道世人，又知道我本分內各事，此大益也。(Answer: As this boy be taught, I would know the true God, myself, humanity, and all my duties, this would be great benefit for me.)

30. Ibid., 16.
31. Ibid., 18.

Questions 114 to 165 were about death and after life, angels, saints, Hell, demons, resurrection, the last judgment, and heaven. Milne's catechism ended with a morning prayer and an evening prayer for the youth. Compared to *The Shorter Catechism* and Willison's *Mother's Catechism*, as regards to theology, Milne's catechism was primarily Calvinistic.

Drawing on his own learning experience during his youth, Milne also instructed parents that "when teaching your child, you shall be aware of his ability, in order for him to understand."[32] For Milne, the purpose of education was for the student to understand; thus for Milne, parents should teach their children with easy texts at first, and then harder ones as the children's understanding advances.[33] This philosophy of education reflects Jonathan Edwards' (1703–1758), who also stressed pupils' understanding of given texts, through which "knowledge is acquired, and thereby choices informed."[34]

AFTER CONVERSION: AN EVANGELICAL SPIRIT

In Milne's personal account, he pointed out that Thomas Boston's sermon "The Soul's Espousals to Christ," and George Cowie's sermon on Revelation 22:21, were critical to his conversion experience.[35] Milne also commented on Cowie's preaching as "evangelical and spiritual," under which he felt "disposed for prayer, saw the evils of my heart, and found the people spiritual and edifying in their conversation."[36]

For people in Huntly and around the region, "the name of Cowie had become . . . a household word," with the impression

---

32. Ibid., 9.
33. Ibid., 9–11.
34. Minkema, "Jonathan Edwards on Education," 33. Also see Bezzant, "Singly, Particularly, Closely"; and Minkema, "Informing of the Child's Understanding."
35. Morrison, *Memoirs*, 8.
36. Ibid., 9.

of his character, and footsteps in preaching the gospel.[37] Cowie, with his own heartfelt conversion experience, he preached with "a peculiar charm, which seldom accompanies that which is the effect of mechanical labour and theoretical study."[38] In Donald Morrison's words,

> [Cowie's] appearance was that of dignified simplicity. He could declaim, and he could be pathetic. His discourse partook of the colloquial. He had studied human nature and he knew how to approach it at every avenue. The power he had over an audience was great beyond description. He could make them smile or weep. His appeal to the conscience was unceremonious and direct. He never lost sight of the theme of the pulpit. . . . He was a stern reprover of sin; but he melted with tenderness over the sinner, beseeching him to be reconciled unto God.[39]

Robert Philip, another parishioner of Cowie, compared Cowie with George Whitefield (1714–1770) in character, and commented

> . . . the majestic music of his voice is yet in my ear, and the angelic benevolence of his countenance yet before my eye. . . . I wept often then because he was bathed in tears of love. I loved him, because he loved me for my father's sake . . .[40]

Meanwhile, Cowie was, as already mentioned, aware of his own soul, as he "he looked well to the paths of his feet, and pondered all his goings."[41] With a "godly jealousy" of his own soul, Cowie searched his heart and mind, and sought an affected "heart-holiness" in Christ.[42] With this passion for the salvation of

---

37. Campbell, "Rev. John Hill," 16.
38. Anonymous, "Memoir of the Late Rev.," 123.
39. Quoted in Haldane, *Memoirs*, 260.
40. Philip, *Life and Times*, 553–54.
41. Anonymous, "Memoir of the Late Rev.," 123.
42. On December 28, 1774, Cowie wrote in his journal: "Alas! I am a poor timorous creature, above many, I believe. Lord, help me, for thy mercies sake! Keep for me, and clear to me that which thou hast given. I am tempted to

Training Laborers for His Harvest

lost souls, Cowie committed himself and his congregation in supporting missions. By inviting and providing pulpit for Anglican minister Rowland Hill (1744–1833) in 1799, and other itinerant preachers, like James Alexander Haldane (1768–1849), John Aikman (1759–1834) and Joseph Rate (1776–1846), as well as by supporting missionary societies, Cowie was deposed and excommunicated by the Antiburgher Synod in 1800.[43]

As Milne attended Sunday schools, worship services, and heard sermons preached under Cowie, it is certain that Milne gained his missionary spirits, and understanding of the church and ministry of a minister from Cowie. With his conversion, Milne's spirituality was enhanced by the influence of Cowie, in particular, Milne's prayer life and self-examination.[44] It is also certain that Milne was influenced by Cowie's style of preaching, as he would later preach Christocentric, simplistic sermons in both

---

think that the faith of hypocrites is operative; yet I believe they are rather rejoiced with the hope of happiness than taken up about heart-holiness. Gospel doctrines may touch their affections, work about their hearts, and produce some things like graces of the Spirit; but they never have their hearts won and renewed; their will itself renewed, quickened, and subjected. They are not sincerely won from sin; they are not brought out of themselves to Christ for righteousness and strength, in any sweet, hearty, and powerful way: their convictions are neither so deep nor so decisive as to make salvation by Christ absolutely necessary. On these accounts I have some hope that my situation is different from that of hypocrites. Therefore,—'Hold fast till I come.'" Anonymous, "Memoir of the Late Rev.," 123.

43. Detailed record on Cowie's excommunication see Kinniburgh, *Fathers of Independency*, 19–22.

44. For instance, in a resolution Milne made for himself on January 1, 1810, he wrote:
1. To spend a little time thrice a day for meditation, prayer, and reading the sacred scriptures, and some devotional book.
2. To spend some extraordinary time every three months for the state of my soul and work.
3. To spend some time on Saturday night, from eight o'clock, in religious exercises for myself, and relations, and friends, in Scotland.
4. To attend as many prayer-meetings as I can, for the benefit of my soul.

Morrison, *Memoirs*, 29.

The Theology of William Milne

English and Chinese. As Milne reminded himself every time before preaching,

1. Remember, O my soul, that thou art now to plead the cause of Christ, therefore be fervent.
2. Remember, that some who shall hear me to day will, perhaps, be in heaven or hell before another opportunity, therefore be faithful.
3. Some are remarkably ignorant, therefore be very plain.
4. Some are captious, therefore be cautious.
5. Some, perhaps, are beginning, tried, tempted, desponding, &c. therefore seek to direct them.
6. What if I never preach again, therefore be as serious as if I were to go from the pulpit to my bed of death.[45]

THEOLOGICAL TRAINING: AN EDWARDSEAN ROOT

At Gosport, David Bogue did not lecture; he wrote outlines of topics, "leaving several inches of space under each heading, and gave a reading list."[46] Students like Milne would be "expected to copy the outline, fill in the intervening spaces, and enter into oral dialogue with Bogue on the results."[47] As an Edwardsean theologian, titles of Edwards' books featured prominently in Bogue's reading list, such as the *Humble Attempt, History of the Work of Redemption*, and *The Life of Brainerd*.[48] Along with reading other theologians, such as Philip Limborch (1633–1712), David Clarkson (1622–1686), John Flavel (1627–1691), John Owen (1616–1683), Thomas Ridgley (1667–1734), Isaac Watts (1674–1748), John Gill (1697–1771), William Wishart (1691/2–1753), and Thomas Boston, the theology "imbibed by Gosport students, then, was predominantly, if not

---

45. Ibid., 32–33.
46. Walls, "Missions," 251.
47. Ibid.
48. Ibid., 252; Frey, *Theological Lectures*, 1:17, 113, 394.

exclusively, Calvinist, Puritan, English nonconformist or Scottish Presbyterian."[49]

Christopher A. Daily has rightfully argued that there are reflections of the missionary strategy of David Bogue in Morrison and Milne's missiological practices; this influence Daily calls the "Gosport template." Yet Daily incorrectly concludes that Bogue's strategy was purely educational, which would mean that the goal of the missionaries was to "put a Gosport-like education into the hands of the Chinese" in establishing a Protestant church in China, and this makes Daily "[call] into question [Morrison and Milne's] originality and their contribution to the overall design of their mission."[50] Daily summarizes Morrison and Milne's methodology thus: they followed the "Gosport template" in three steps, which are learning the Chinese language, doing literary work (including translation, printing and distributing), and setting up a school (*i.e.*, Anglo-Chinese College).[51]

Though Daily's argument was based on decent archival research, he erroneously over-valued academy education against the evangelistic-core of missionary work. Such argumentation suggests a lack of understanding in regard to doctrines such as conversion—in particular justification and regeneration—and ecclesiology. If Daily's argument is correct, then it contradicts Bogue's understanding of overseas mission and missionary education, as well as Milne's own account of missiological methods presented at his ordination service.[52] Bogue argued that "the sole business of a missionary is to promote the religion of Jesus," which is the same task as that of a local minister of the gospel.[53] By making such a statement, Bogue shows that he understood that "the

---

49. Piggin, *Making Evangelical Missionaries*, 176.

50. Daily, *Robert Morrison*, 11, 13, 198, 199.

51. Daily, "From Gosport to Canton," 170–297.

52. Morrison, *Memoirs*, 16–19.

53. Bogue, *Objections Against a Mission*, 11. In this sermon, Bogue sought to answer ten objections concerning the necessity and possibility of foreign missions, and concluded that Christians should depend on God wholeheartedly in fulfilling the Great Commission by sending qualified missionaries overseas to preach the gospel of Jesus Christ.

The Theology of William Milne

main object of the foreign missionary enterprise is to establish the church in each non-Christian land."[54] Bogue further argued that, as such, the gospel task is authorized by Jesus Christ who "has all power, both in heaven and in earth," and who "has assured us, that He came to be a light to enlighten the heathen, as well as to be the glory of his people Israel."[55] Jesus Christ, Bogue understood, is the "foundation of our hope," and the missionaries' "sole dependence" of success.[56] Thus, for Bogue, "the academy [is] an instrument of evangelism," which means Gosport was a place providing theological training for young men, who were carefully chosen by the missionary committee, in order to be ready for their missionary task.[57] It is no surprise that,

> no one could leave [Bogue's] Gosport [academy] without a deep impression of the grandeur and responsibility of the ministry and an awful anticipation of the day when each shepherd of souls must render up his account to the Good Shepherd who laid down His life for the sheep.[58]

Thus, when missionaries like Morrison and Milne were participating in various literary works and establishing academies in

---

54. Brown, *Rising Churches*, 23.

55. Bogue, *Objections Against a Mission*, 5.

56. Ibid. Bogue's argument about dependence on God in missions is common to his contemporary theologians, such as the Baptists of the time, since such argument had been consistently brought back by Joshua Marshman (1768–1837) and Christopher Anderson (1782–1852) after the death of Andrew Fuller, who argued that the directors of the Baptist Missionary Society should rediscover "the spirit of individual exertion," which means both the missionary societies and the missionaries themselves should depend simply on God, rather than "on vast means acquired by impressive (voluntary) mission societies." Moreover, "spiritual renewal must replace a secular mind-set in the BMS committee." Smith, "Edinburgh Connection," 191–92.

57. In David Bogue's missionary lectures, he has five points of missionary qualifications, which are (1) natural qualifications (such as good temper); (2) knowledge (of doctrine, of the heart, of customs); (3) spiritual disposition (there are ten examples in total, for instance, peculiar affection for souls); (4) generous, liberal principles; and (5) continued aims and ends. Noel Gibbard, "David Bogue," 38, 39.

58. Bennett, *Memoirs*, 130–31.

their mission fields, their purpose was to provide literary resources for teaching in the academy in order to train indigenous pastors who would be able to read and understand both Chinese and English literature--specifically the Scriptures--in their own language and with Christian principles.[59] This makes the academy not "a storehouse where knowledge was heaped up, but a channel of blessing to those in need."[60] In this way, the Anglo-Chinese College, following the patterns of Bogue's Gosport academy, provided "a residential environment for Chinese students . . . and European students . . . to learn together," under the banner of the Christian worldview, in order to engage their minds.[61]

By the same token, Morrison and Milne can be called Edwardsean missionaries, inasmuch as Bogue was "a good representative of [Jonathan] Edwards' indirect influence [on mission]."[62] As Stuart Piggin claims, "Jonathan Edwards was massively constitutive of modern Protestant missions." He argues that there are at least seven facets in Edwards' "missionary diamond": theology; history (role of providence in history); philosophy (free will and nature of virtue); pragmatics (missionary strategy, including prayer, examples of individual conversion, and theological education); practice ("duty and evidencing of conversion by fruit"), spirituality (religious affections), and aesthetics ("nature enthusiasm and

---

59. In his proposal to the LMS directors, Robert Morrison wrote that the Anglo-Chinese College existed "for the purpose of teaching English and the principles of the Christian religion to Chinese youth, and particularly for the purpose of instructing missionaries and others in the language and literature of China" (Harrison, *Waiting for China*, 35). As Morrison and Milne hoped that the Anglo-Chinese College would be "the reciprocal cultivation of Chinese and European Literature," and "it is hoped that this course of proceeding will ultimately have a favorable influence on the peaceable diffusion of Christian principles, and the general civilization of the eastern hemisphere." (Morrison, *Memoirs*, 1:513; Hancock, *Robert Morrison*, 137–38). It is clear, for Morrison and Milne, "human knowledge is the means; the acquisition of Divine knowledge is the end" (Morrison, *To the Public*, 3).

60. Gibbard, "David Bogue," 39–40.

61. Hancock, *Robert Morrison*, 139.

62. Walls, "Missions," 251.

The Theology of William Milne

sensibility tantalizingly adumbrative of Romanticism").[63] Each of these deserves brief explanation in regard to how it had influenced Bogue, but the emphasis here is specifically on the two facets of theology-philosophy and practice.

Theologically and philosophically, based on the doctrines of sin and grace, Jonathan Edwards' *Freedom of the Will* (1754) "exerted the greatest force on evangelical theology," as it rediscovered "indiscriminate evangelism" in the Great Awakening, in which

> "Edwards provided an analysis of the freedom of the will that distinguished between a non-elect sinner's 'natural ability'... to repent and turn from sin, and his or her 'moral inability'... to do the same."[64] By distinguishing man's free will, Edwards emphasizes "the sovereignty of God [which] postulates the decree and act of God in redeeming the sinner."[65]

Understanding man's total depravity, and God's irresistible grace, Edwards would preach the gospel and lead people to God through faith in Christ. Along with Edwards, Bogue would argue that the gospel mission is theocentric in its motive, content, authority, purpose, means, and success.[66] It is the missionaries' duty

> to make [the pagan] feel his miserable state as a sinner, and to lead him to a cordial acceptance of Christ, as

63. Walls, "Missions," 266–96.

64. Sweeney and Withrow explain that "indiscriminate evangelism" means "the revivalists' practice of extending the gospel promises to everyone, without stressing that God redeems only those elected for salvation." Sweeney and Withrow, "Jonathan Edwards," 297.

65. Turnbull, *Jonathan Edwards the Preacher*, 143.

66. For a detailed examination on Bogue's mission motives see Terpstra, "David Bogue," 271–322. Based on Johannes Van Den Berg's ten classifications of missionary motivations (Van Den Berg, *Constrained by Jesus' Love*; A summary of Van Ben Berg's arguments see George, "Evangelical Revival," 58–63), the motivations of the eighteenth-century missionaries and their agencies are political, humanitarian-cultural, ascetic, a sense of indebtedness, romantic, theocentric, love and compassion, ecclesiological, eschatological, and the command of Christ. Terpstra carefully examines the impact of Bogue's doctrines of God, man, Christology, soteriology, eschatology, and ecclesiology on his mission motives, which identified his Edwardsean characteristics.

made of God unto him, "wisdom, righteousness, sanctification, and redemption." It is to bring him from the love of the world to a supreme love to God, as his Creator, Redeemer, and Sanctifier. It is to draw him away from the indulgence of divers lusts and pleasures, which reigned in his soul, and from all the impurities of a [p]agan conversion, to a life of unreserved and universal obedience to the will of God. It is to lead him from the stupid adoration of stocks and stones, and the senseless, impure, or sanguinary rites of the Heathen mythology, to worship the Father in spirit and in truth, and to render to him the homage of a pure heart, wholly devoted to his service.[67]

Thus, Bogue would assert that a missionary has "Jesus his Master at his right-hand, accompanying him on the way, and the Holy Spirit resting on him like a flame of fire, with all his powerful energies" in preaching the gospel and living according to their message.[68]

Practically, evidence also indicates that Bogue was an Edwardsean, particularly in his theological education. In a letter to Sir William Pepperrell (1696–1759) in November 1751, Jonathan Edwards explained his philosophy of education. Here Edwards advocated a dialogical method in order to teach pupils both "things" and "words."[69] In practice, Edwards argued that after a pupil finished reading some material, the teacher should not only explain the words and content of the material, but also turn it into an open conversation based on the reading "with 'familiar questions' that encourage the child 'to speak freely, and in his turn also to ask questions, for the solution of his own doubts.'"[70] Edwards argued that by helping the student to gain a "habit of conversation," the pupil would begin reflecting on and understanding divine matters.[71] In theological education, as Edwards applied this dialogic method in his mentorship to several ministerial candidates, he also understood

67. Bogue, *Objections*, 5–6.
68. Ibid., 15–18.
69. Minkema, "Jonathan Edwards on Education," 32.
70. Ibid.
71. Ibid., 32–33.

The Theology of William Milne

the importance of the spiritual formation for them. This Edwardsean pastoral educational formula was preserved and continuously practiced by Edwards' student Joseph Bellemy (1718–1790) in his seminary at Bethlehem, Connecticut, which was a combination of "the study of speculative divinity with practical piety."[72] This kind of theological education can also be found in Bogue's Gosport academy, and would later by used by Milne in his mentorship of Liang Fa, which will be analyzed later in the next chapter.

Bogue taught an Edwardsean missiological method which is identical to that of another Edwardsean missionary--William Carey, whose method Stephen Neil summarizes in five points: "widespread preaching of the gospel by every possible method, distributing the Bible in the languages of the people, establishing a church as soon as possible, studying the background and worldviews of the people, and training indigenous leaders."[73] Even if they were unaware of it, it is certainly not a coincidence for Carey, Morrison, and Milne, to use a similar missiological method, since they all came from the same Edwardsean root.

In conclusion, the "Gosport template," which Robert Morrison and William Milne took and practiced in China, was rooted in Edwardsean Calvinism, which taught the missionaries to declare "a single gospel for all humanity without distinction of race or religious profession," acquainted with deep understanding of indigenous culture, in order to lead people to conversion, "a requirement for all."[74] Genuine conversion is thus foundational to the theological training

---

72. Hensley, "Bellamy, Joseph," 43. On Edwards' spiritual formation see Lucas, "Man Just Like Us," 29–41; Whitney, "Pursuing a Passion for God, 109–28; and Beck, *Voice of Faith*, 55–71, 211–66. On Joseph Bellamy's education see Conforti, "Joseph Bellamy," 126–38; Conforti, "Rise of the New Divinity," 37–47.

73. Neill, *History of Christian Missions*, 224. In his essay, Kenneth B. Mulholland argued that these five points of missiological method were built on the Reformation platform made up of three planks, which were Pietism, Moravianism, and Puritanism. Mulholland, "From Luther to Carey," 85–95. On the Baptist mission see Young, "Andrew Fuller," 17–27; Oussoren, *William Carey*; Smith, "Tale of Many Models," 479–500. Also compare Piggin, *Making Evangelical Missionaries*, 178–81.

74. Walls, "Missions," 260.

Training Laborers for His Harvest

of indigenous leaders in the church.[75] This was what Milne learned from Bogue at Gosport, and practiced in China.

IN MISSION FIELD: A SCHOLAR-PASTOR

Though he received his theological training and liberal education at Gosport, Milne had to study Chinese, the native language of those he was sent to evangelize, when he arrived. This, according to Bogue, was the first duty of a missionary, and "a spiritual service acceptable to God through Jesus Christ."[76] After many years of hard labor in studying the Chinese language, and

> with an eye for detail, a capacity for vision, a sharp tongue, and an acute awareness that China had "persecuting edicts and an almost unconquerable jealousy of strangers," Milne became seriously proficient in Chinese (satisfying even Morrison's exalted standards).[77]

His ability in using Chinese can also be reflected in his translation of a few Old Testament books from Hebrew to Chinese, as well as his tracts in Chinese.

Along with studying Chinese, Milne also had to read and study various religions in China, including Daoism, Buddhism, Confucianism, and folk religions. In his *Memoirs*, Morrison recorded Milne's short writings on various Chinese religious topics. In every issue of the Indo-Chinese Gleaner, Milne gave detailed studies on particular religious topics in China and Malacca. These studies helped Morrison and Milne not to fall into the same error

---

75. David Bebbington summarized four marks of evangelicalism: (1) conversionism, "the belief that lives need to be changed;" (2) activism, "the expression of the gospel in effort;" (3) biblicism, "a particular regard for the Bible;" (4) crucicentrism, "a stress on the sacrifice of Christ on the cross" (Bebbington, *Evangelism in Modern Britain*, 7). For Jonathan Edwards, "the conversion of any soul depended on God's decision, and the pastor's duty was to remain available for God to use as a tool in the work of redemption" (Kidd, *Great Awakening*, 16).

76. Piggin, *Making Evangelical Missionaries*, 177.

77. Hancock, *Robert Morrison*, 136.

The Theology of William Milne

of syncretism of the Nestorians, who used Buddhist and Daoist terminologies without any change. Rather, Morrison and Milne tried to understand Chinese words and terms linguistically, and sought to communicate Christian doctrines without syncretizing it to paganism. One of the best examples of their careful use of Chinese language is their decision on the name of God in Chinese.

Unlike the Nestorians who created a new Chinese name, Zhen zhu (真主, lit. "True Lord"), or the Roman Catholics who used Tian zhu (天主, lit. "Heavenly Lord"), Morrison and Milne used Shen (神) from 1813 in Morrison's New Testament, which they believed "was a more generic term, meaning gods, God, spirit, or soul, and that they could destroy Chinese gods by using the Christian Shen."[78] Even though Walter H. Medhurst (1796–1857) later argued that "the word Shen had never referred to the Supreme God" in Confucian literature, and concluded that Shangdi (上帝, lit. Sovereign on High) "was the substance (體 *ti*) of Shen, and Shen was the spiritual function (用 *yong*) of Shangdi," Shen was used by most American missionaries like Elijah C. Bridgman (1801–1861). As Archie C. C. Lee pointed out that by insisting on the generic term Shen, the translators "were convinced that the Chinese did not have any knowledge of the Creator God in Christianity and that therefore was obviously no equivalent term to represent the notion of a monotheistic God."[79] This was the same conviction Morrison and Milne took. In a recent comparative study on the terms Shangdi and Shen, linguist G. Wright Doyle presented the advantages and disadvantages of both terms, and concluded by suggesting the use of Shen in "most preaching and teaching, and in all translations of the Bible," as it "being the most accurate rendering of *Elohim* and of *Theos*," and only to use Shangdi when "it is adequately explained according to the full Biblical revelation."[80] It is certain that by choosing the name of God in Chinese, Milne was forced to understand both the doctrine of God, and the Chinese language and culture.

78. Oak, "Competing Chinese Names," 94.
79. Lee, "God's Asian Names."
80. Doyle, "Names for 'God.'"

4

The Mentorship of Liang Fa

As has been presented in previous chapters, eighteenth-century Protestant missionaries came to China in a different historical context with a different missiological method in comparison with the Nestorian and the Roman Catholic missionaries of the previous centuries. With the understanding of Milne's theology, in this chapter, one of the Protestant missiological methods--mentorship--will be examined, in order to prove that mentorship was the most effective missiological method in Morrison and Milne's historical setting and theological framework.

DISCIPLESHIP AND MENTORSHIP

It is both necessary and helpful to explain the usage of the terms of "discipleship" and "mentorship" prior to further exploration of Milne's mentorship of Liang Fa, since there are confusions of the meanings of the words in today's context.

Biblically, the word "discipleship/disciple" occurs more than eighty-nine times in the New Testament, and is used to designate "one as a believer in Jesus," and thus "all true believers are

The Mentorship of Liang Fa

disciples."[1] Based on biblical texts, Michael J. Wilkins further defines the word: "discipleship means the beginning of a new life in intimate fellowship with a living Master and Savior . . . [which] also involves a commitment to call others to such relationship with Jesus Christ."[2] This fellowship is offered by Jesus Christ to his believers in such a way that they have "personal relationship with himself," and its ultimate goal is for them "to be conformed to Jesus' image," and "live out a life of witness in word and deed to the world that Jesus is Lord."[3] Such growth takes place in the community of disciples, which is the church, and is a "wholistic" and life-long process.[4] Theologically, discipleship has been significant to Christians throughout the ages, and as a result, it has been understood in various ways.[5] However, it is essential to understand that discipleship must be done "in the coordinates of the theology of the cross and justification, seeking neither to downplay suffering . . . nor to become absorbed in it."[6] In other words, discipleship is intimately tied with conversion, which ought to be characterized by its genuineness.

On the other hand, though the word "mentor" or "mentoring" does not occur in the New Testament, the meaning of mentorship is found in various texts. Today, the meaning of mentoring varies in different cultural contexts, but Edward L. Smither argues that "mentoring in essence means that a master, expert, or someone with significant experience is imparting knowledge and skill to a novice in an atmosphere of discipline, commitment, and accountability."[7]

---

1. Wilkins, "Disciple, Discipleship," 279.

2. Ibid. Detailed exegetical study on discipleship see Wilkins, *Discipleship in the Ancient World*.

3. Wilkins, "Disciple, Discipleship," 279.

4. Ibid., 280.

5. For a theological survey of historical understanding of discipleship see Starke, "Discipleship," 1:851–53.

6. Ibid., 1:853. Also see Bonhoeffer, *Cost of Discipleship*; Longenecker, *Patterns of Discipleship*; Di Gangi, *Meaning of Christian Discipleship*.

7. Smither, *Augustine as Mentor*, 4.

Training Laborers for His Harvest

Thus, for Smither, mentoring and discipleship are interchangeable terms, since according to the New Testament and early Christian writings, mentoring or discipleship is "the work of one Christian helping another disciple or group of disciples grow in their knowledge and application of the teachings of Jesus and the Scriptures."[8] Based on Smither's definition, mentorship in this book is specifically referring to training future leaders in the church, which means the making of such a mentorship relationship is found in discipleship. In other words, both the mentor and the protégé commit to and practice the shared belief in Jesus Christ. This mentoring leadership development has been practiced by the apostle Paul in his church-planting ministry, as he invested his life in men like Timothy and Titus. By studying Paul's mentorship of Timothy, Chuck Lawless argues that mentoring should continue today "to be a primary method of leadership development."[9] Lawless summarizes Paul's mentorship in five ways:

> First, Paul took the lead in establishing the mentoring relationships . . . [that is] the leader led the way in calling out the next generation of leaders.[10]
>
> Second, leadership development through mentoring produced a profound connection between Paul and Timothy. . . . Leadership development was thus much more than a program; it was a relationship.[11]
>
> Third, Paul recognized Timothy's areas of needed growth . . . and Paul encouraged . . . reminded . . . suggest . . . [and] warned [Timothy].[12]
>
> Fourth, Paul invited Timothy into his life. [Thus, as] Timothy learned from Paul on the mountaintop and in the valley . . . it was in the context of . . . life-on-life leadership development.[13]

---

8. Ibid., 12.

9. Lawless, "Paul and Leadership Development," 233. Also see Hoehl, "Mentor Relationships," 32–47.

10. Lawless, "Paul and Leadership Development," 227–28.

11. Ibid., 228.

12. Ibid., 229.

13. Ibid., 229–30.

The Mentorship of Liang Fa

Fifth, Paul challenged Timothy to fulfill his own calling... Knowing that Timothy was gifted... Paul trained him, sent him out to do ministry and often reconnected with him between tasks. [This mentorship] continued until the mentor died.[14]

Thus, mentoring leadership development is essential in both local churches and on mission fields. Based on their study of Paul's approach, Henry Venn (1796–1873) and Rufus Anderson (1796–1880), and later John L. Nevius (1829–1893), argued that missionaries should "train national pastors and hand the care of the churches over to them at the earliest opportunities," in order to plant a "three-self" church, that is a church "would be self-supporting, self-governing and self-propagating."[15] With the completion of translating the Bible into Chinese, this "hand over" of the church to indigenous pastors was possible for Morrison and Milne.

"BUT GOD ONLY CAN MAKE A MINISTER"— EXPLORING MILNE'S MENTORSHIP OF LIANG[16]

As Edwardsean missionaries, Morrison and Milne understood the core task of their mission was to make disciples of Jesus Christ among the Chinese, and as a result, they sought opportunities to evangelize both large groups of people and individuals such as Cai Gao (or Tsae a-ko, who was the first Chinese Protestant convert, baptized on July 16, 1814 by Robert Morrison), Cai's two brothers, and Liang Fa, whom Morrison and Milne hired for the printing press. By faithful presentation of the gospel in both their words and life examples, Morrison and Milne eagerly hoped that God might let them see the fruits of Chinese conversion, which is the

---

14. Ibid., 230–33; Hoehl, "Mentor Relationships," 35.

15. Terry, "Paul and Indigenous Missions," 165–66. On practicing this Pauline missionary strategy see Hesselgrave, *Planting Churches Cross-Culturally*; Wright, *Practical Theology of Missions*.

16. The complete sentence of the quote is "That man may make a preacher, but God only can make a minister." Cowie, *Dissenter's Guide*, 8.

Training Laborers for His Harvest

work of the Holy Spirit.[17] Yet, Chinese native conversion is not the only end--for Morrison and Milne were not only seeking to disciple new converts, but also to mentor them for ministerial business, so that the gospel might be brought to mainland China by Chinese themselves.[18] As an exploration of Milne's mentorship of Liang, the following section aims to answer two questions: first, how exactly Milne led Liang to conversion, and second, how he mentored Liang for future ministerial leadership.

Pathway to Conversion

From the biographical sketch in chapter 2, it is clear that it was under Morrison's influence and through his labor in making the New Testament blocks, that Liang Fa became a seeker of Christian faith; this was soon after he arrived Malacca with Milne.[19] After rejecting Buddhism, Liang "began to recite the prayers" and sat under Milne's sermons.[20] McNeur records Liang's testimony of his journey toward the recognition of his sin and of his need of Jesus the Savior:

> . . . I heard the missionary [William Milne] preach the doctrine of atonement through Jesus, and at my leisure I examined the Scriptures . . . Then I thought "These

---

17. Philip, *Life and Opinion*, 111.

18. One example of Morrison and Milne's desire to mentor and train future Chinese ministers is reflected in Morrison's report to the LMS in January 1816, when he wrote concerning Cai Gao, who was the first convert Morrison baptized in 1814: "A-fo, or properly Tsae A-fo (Tsae, being the sacred or family name, is not used generally), whom I baptized, continues to make conscience of attending on the Lord's day at worship. He is not so docile as I could wish." This was the first time in one and a half years, that is, since Cai Gao's baptism, that he was mentioned. Su Ching explains that it is "probably because A-ko [Cai Gao] had not made remarkable progress in his faith regarding both doctrinal understanding and moral character." Ching, "First Protestant Convert of China," 239. On Morrison's dissatisfaction of Cai Gao also see McNeur, *China's First Preacher*, 21–22.

19. McNeur, *China's First Preacher*, 23; Li, *History of Early Christian Missionary*, 175, n. 17; Bohr, "Liang Fa's Quest," 36–40.

20. McNeur, *China's First Preacher*, 24.

The Mentorship of Liang Fa

are good books, exhorting men to depart from iniquity. Moreover the doctrines are attested by the miracles of Jesus, therefore the book must certainly be true." I then listened to the expounding of the Scriptures, and on the Sabbath read the Bible more attentively, requesting the missionary [Milne] to explain it to me. I asked what was meant by Jesus making atonement for sin. The missionary [Milne] told me that Jesus was the Son of God sent into the world to suffer for the sins of men in order that all who believe in Him might obtain salvation. Feeling myself to be a sinner I asked how I was to obtain pardon. The missionary [Milne] said, "If you believe in Jesus Christ [he] will receive you as His adopted son, and in the world to come bestow on you everlasting life." . . . On returning to my room I thought with myself "I am a great sinner, and if I do not depend on the merits of Christ how can God forgive me?" I then determined to become a disciple of Jesus and requested baptism.[21]

Though there is no recorded report of the conversations between Milne and Liang on questions Liang had about God, Scripture, sin, and salvation, it is certain that Milne spent time answering Liang's questions concerning the gospel truth with patience, and walked with Liang along his way as he sought his Savior. Liang was baptized by Milne in 1816. Three years later, in 1819 at Malacca, Milne wrote and published *Dialogues Between Chang and Yuen* (張遠兩友相論), a novelistic and catechistic tract based on the conversations of a Chang, who is a Christian, and a Yuen, Chang's heathen neighbor. The contents of these dialogues between these two friends are summarized by Milne as:

> 1. Questions proposed by Yuen concerning Christian principles and character; the being of God. 2. Evangelical repentance. 3. Character of Christ, and faith in him. 4. Good men seek their chief happiness in heaven; annihilation of the soul considered. 5. Chang relates his first acquaintance with the New Testament. 6. Yuen having retired, is struck with horror at his own neglect of the true God; visits Chang and finds him with his family at

---

21. Ibid., 24–25.

prayer; the resurrection of the dead. 7. Nature and qualities of the raised bodies; doubts and objections. 8. Yuen on visiting Chang in the evening, finds him in his closet, which leads to a discussion on the object, and kinds of prayer; worshipping the dead, &c. 9. The awful judgment to come; a midnight prayer under the Woo-tung tree. 10. Yuen objects to Chang's last night's prayer, be cause he confessed himself to be a sinner; 11. Yuen deeply impressed with the ideas of eternity of sin, spends a whole night in his garden, bewailing his miserable condition. 12. Chang explains to him the method of salvation by Jesus Christ; the felicity of heaven; and misery of hell.[22]

Historically, Milne's *Dialogues* constituted the first missionary novel in common Chinese, and became the most famous and best-selling Christian tract in China. The work received a wild reading, since it was not only famous among the Chinese, but also was translated and sold in Korea, where it had significant influence upon the church.[23]

Although Milne's *Dialogues* had been reprinted and revised various times after its first publication, until recently there have been few academic studies done on the tract.[24] Most of these studies are conducted from a literary perspective; in other words, scholars are interested in the literary value of the tract. By neglecting Milne's and the tract's historical and theological context, they assume that this tract is completely fictional, and that by choosing to use this kind of genre, Milne aimed at attracting Chinese readers. Comparing Milne's *Dialogues* with Liang's personal testimony concerning his conversion, it is not hard to figure out the similari-

22. Milne, *Retrospect*, 281–82.

23. Sung-Deuk Oak noticed the influence of Milne's *Dialogues* in the conversion of Kil Sonju (1869–1935), "one of the first seven Presbyterian ministers ordained in 1907." Oak, *Making of Korean Christianity*, 246–50, 251–52, 283–84. Also see Oh, "Spread and Translation," 215–50.

24. Most studies are on an introductory level without deep analytical and theological study. See Hanan, *Chinese Fiction*, 58–61; Song, *Chinese Missionary Novel*, 60–77; Song, "Modern Development," 57–62; and Song, "First Chinese Missionary Novel." For a more detailed theological study see Bays, "Christian Tracts," 19–34.

The Mentorship of Liang Fa

ties of the content. In many cases, Liang was in a similar situation to Yuan, as both of them were interested in Christianity, burdened with sin, and were counseled by Christian friends (especially compare *Dialogues* chapter ten, Yuen's reflection on sin). Thus it is clear that Milne's *Dialogues* is not completely fictional; rather, it communicates the method Milne used in leading Liang to Christ. Milne's *Dialogues* is evangelistic in its nature.

On the basis of the conversations of Pan Chang (潘長) and Cao Yuen (曹遠), three evangelistic characteristics can be observed that are possibly applied by Milne in conversing with Liang. First, there is clear communication of the gospel in conversation. In *Dialogues* chapter 1, after a very brief introduction of the setting, Milne wrote about Chang's explanation of the uniqueness of Christians in their ways of worshiping the one true and only God (真的惟一上帝, lit., "true and only supreme ruler"), and acknowledgment of one's depraved nature which leads to one's eager desire for redemption (信耶穌者皆知自己有罪，苦心懺悔).[25] For Chang, it is clear that "there is but one only living and true God," who is the Creator, the origin of all things (天地萬物之原本是也, lit., "origin of everything in heaven and on earth").[26] The attributes of God are his sovereignty (全能), omniscience (至智), mercy (至恩), righteousness (至義), holiness (至聖), and grace (至憐).[27] In nature, the true living God is one God in three persons (上帝止一，但其體有三位, lit., "the supreme ruler is only one, but in the unity of the Godhead there are three persons"), namely the Father (聖父, lit., "Holy Father"), Son (聖子, lit., "Holy Son")

25. Milne, *Dialogues*, 5, 7.

26. Westminster Assembly of Divines, "Westminster Confession," 3:606. In answering Yuen's question concerning the difference between God and heaven (which is a term substitute for "God" in common Chinese idiom. For instance, 天子 [lit., "son of heaven"] is the title used to emperor, which refers the emperor's divine right), Chang explains with an illustration of the difference between a table and a craftsman, and points out that "heaven is created, but God is the Creator (天是受造之物，上帝是造物主也)." Milne, *Dialogues*, 6.

27. Noticing the use of Chinese adjective "至" ("most") in describing God's attributes, which makes the translation literally be: God is sovereign, most wise, most merciful, most righteous, most holy, and most gracious. Milne, *Dialogues*, 6.

and Holy Spirit (聖神, lit., "Holy Spirit").[28] These three persons are not three gods, but one God.[29] The second person of the triune God is called Jesus, which is a "foreign" name, which means "save," this name was given to the Son of God since he came into the world to save people.[30] Chang clearly points out that Jesus and God are one in nature and Godhead (or "wholeness;" 耶穌與上帝一性一體), and share in the same divine attributes (至聖全能是也, lit., "he is most holy and sovereign").[31]

Concerning humanity, Chang points out in the conversations, that men are morally depraved, which means, that man's heart is evil (惡), and what is worse, men do not know their iniquities.[32] Chang further tells Yuen that "all have sinned against God," and that the destiny for sinners is to suffer the eternal punishment of hell.[33] Chang points out that "repentance is the path to the Truth," and for those who believe in Jesus, God is gracious, and their sins are forgiven.[34] Chang further explains in chapter 2 that it is only through the atonement of Jesus, that sins can be forgiven; Jesus' atonement is penal and substitutionary (代萬人受難 lit., "[he]

---

28. It was not easy for early missionaries to translate theological terms into Chinese. The choice of the word "體" for the word Godhead is wise, since the word literally means "a whole set, wholeness," thus the unity of the three persons in the Godhead is communicated. The word "位" is a word of measurement (it expresses a quantity), and is used particularly in reference to humans, and the word is rightfully chosen to communicate the meaning of "being," or "substantive reality." Concerning the translation of the name "Holy Spirit," Milne did not follow the Nestorian and Roman Catholic translation, which translated literally as "original/abstruse wind," or "pure wind." Rather, Milne used the word "神." When "神" is used as a noun, there are multiple possible meanings in classical Chinese, which are (1) deity, (2) spirit, mind, or vigor, and (3) look or expression. The use, which refers to the Holy Spirit, then carries a meaning of a combination of "deity" and "spirit and mind." Milne, *Dialogues*, 10. On the translation of theological terms in Chinese Bible versions see Foley, *Biblical Translation*, 5–34.

29. Milne, *Dialogues*, 10.

30. Ibid.

31. Ibid., 11.

32. Ibid., 9.

33. Ibid., 10.

34. Ibid.

suffered as a substitute for many;" 以贖人罪 lit., "in order to redeem man from sin;" 甘心代我受之 lit., "[he] willingly take place of my suffering").[35] Chang clearly teaches Yuen that conversion is the work of God, the Holy Spirit in particular.[36] Overall, for Milne, it is essential to communicate the gospel faithfully to people, regardless of whether contradictory to people's worldviews or not.

Second, Chang witnessed to Yuen by a Christian example, which means Chang's lifestyle was coherent with his faith. Though Milne chose the catechistical genre in writing this tract, *Dialogues* is not a catechism, since the gospel was not simply communicated verbally in the conversations of Chang and Yuen; the gospel is also witnessed by the way Chang lives both in public and in private. In public, Chang has an excellent reputation, since "everyone knows he is a good and honest person (人人都說他是個善良之人)," and is known to "do good daily (日日行善)."[37] Chang also comments on his change that is after his conversion, he no longer does things that do not please God, for instance, idolatry, drunkenness, adultery, lying, and fraudulence.[38] When approaching people, Chang was not only "always being prepared to make a defense to anyone who asks . . . for a reason for the hope that is in [him]" (1 Pet 3:15), he also does it "with gentleness and respect" (1 Pet 3:16), as is demonstrated by his humble tone of expression, and several special words which were used repeatedly, such as *junjia* (尊駕, lit., "honored sir," which is a very respectable way to address "you" in classical Chinese) and *qigan* (豈敢, lit., "you flatter me").

In private, Chang devotes himself to pursuing growth in God. In chapter 4, Chang shares some impacts from Scripture reading.[39] In chapter 12, toward the end of the tract, Chang introduced Yuen to reading the New Testament, and held a small Bible study with Yuen on John 3:15.[40] Chang is also a man of prayer.

35. Ibid., 13.
36. Ibid., 6, 15, 17, 42.
37. Ibid., 45.
38. Ibid., 7.
39. Ibid., 26.
40. Ibid., 56–57.

Through his personal devotion and public prayers (Chang leads a prayer with Yuen in chapter 8), Chang sets up a model for Yuen. Another practice that influenced Yuen was Chang's family worship (chapters 5 and 7). This second evangelistic characteristic of the *Dialogues* reflects Milne's understanding of how to witness to unbelievers, that is to live the message he wanted others to believe, and to approach people in love.

Third, in Chang's conversation with Yuen, whenever he comes to apologetic matters, Chang uses a presuppositionalistic method. Though the term "presuppositionalism" was not yet invented at Milne's time, through the dialogues between Chang and Yuen, it is certain that Milne understood and applied what is today called presuppositionalism in apologetic practices. First, Milne understood that no one is neutral, for everyone is committed to a worldview. In *Dialogues*, Milne clearly distinguished the Christian worldview from heathen worldviews. For those who follow Jesus, they worship the one true living God, but for the world, they worship "manmade useless idols" (人工所作，無用無能的偶像, lit., "made by man's labor, useless and disabled idol").[41] It is also because of this unique theocentric worldview that Chang cannot tolerate the idea of making heaven--a creature--equally to be called God, who is the Creator.[42] For Milne, even though he borrowed some heathen terms to make the message understandable to the Chinese, his core message of the gospel has never been affected, changed or watered down.

Milne also understood that revelation is the foundation of all knowledge. In *Dialogues* chapter 2, when explaining the meaning of faith, Chang points out that "God issued the Holy Book, expressing to us the understanding of our sins, knowing our unrighteousness, sincerely have faith in Jesus in order to be saved, that we do not rely on ourselves . . . but on Jesus alone . . . (上帝傳下聖書，明示我凡實知自罪，覺自己不義，真心信耶穌以得救，不賴自己 . . . 獨賴耶穌)."[43] By such understanding, Chang

---

41. Ibid., 6.
42. Ibid., 7.
43. Ibid., 14.

The Mentorship of Liang Fa

used both general revelation (for instance, Chang used a bird as an illustration to explain spirit and body in chapter 3, and used the creation of the stars in chapter 4) and special revelation (quoting from the Scripture, and leading Yuen to read the Scripture) to help Yuen to establish a worldview, a worldview for which the "primary ontological axiom is the one living God, and [the] primary epistemological axiom is divine revelation."[44]

Furthermore, it is clear that Chang converses with Yuen with the conviction that all people are without excuse for their rebellion against God, since all people know God by means of general revelation. Chang points out from the beginning that all have sinned in failing to worship the only true one and living God.[45] Though Yuen warns Chang that people might not be pleased with what he is saying about sin, Chang keeps his conviction. This conviction of total depravity is hard for Yuen to understand, since he thought Chang is righteous because he lived a moral life, but Chang replies, "man looks on the outward appearance, but the Lord looks on the heart" (1 Sam 16:7).[46] This conviction asserts what is proven in Milne's *Dialogues*, that a heathen worldview is not and cannot be self-consistent.

In conclusion, through this brief study of the evangelistic characteristics of Milne's *Dialogues Between Chang and Yuen*, it can be seen that Milne understood the importance of conversion. Milne then followed the Pauline example in evangelism that is "going out in love, as Christ's agent in the world, to teach sinners the truth of the gospel with a view to converting and saving them."[47] Such evangelism acknowledges the sovereignty of God, which according to David Bogue implies missionaries are honored to be God's "instruments for conveying the knowledge of salvation to those miserable nations, which are sitting in darkness and in the shadow of death."[48]

44. Henry, *Toward a Recovery*, 49.
45. Milne, *Dialogues*, 6.
46. Ibid., 45–46.
47. Packer, *Evangelism*, 56.
48. Bogue, *Objections*, 4.

Training Laborers for His Harvest

Training of His Chinese Brother

Edward L. Smither describes a Christian mentorship in this way: "the mentor coached his disciples toward realizing the fullness of their salvation."[49] Based on the Scriptures, Smither suggests eight characteristics of mentorship, which are: in the context of a group; the mentor is as a disciple in continual learning; the mentor selects disciple(s) to join in growth and service; the mentor-disciple relationship is personal with both discipline and grace; the mentor teaches sound doctrines; the mentor models and is involved in ministry for imitation; the mentor increases ministerial opportunities for the disciples; and the mentor is always being a "resource or consultant, providing encouragement and perhaps practical advice."[50]

Though William Milne lived only another six years after he baptized Liang Fa and though during these six years Liang left Milne twice for China, Milne's mentorship of Liang was influential and kindled in Liang's heart the same fire that burned in Milne's, a fire that caused Robert Morrison to write of Milne, "a more zealous evangelist never existed."[51] After his baptism, Liang continued working as a printer for Milne, but Milne saw Liang "no longer as a bondservant but more than a bondservant, as a beloved brother" (Phlm 16).[52] As Milne prayed that Liang would "be made faithful unto death," Milne used "some private means" to "increase his knowledge, to impress his heart more deeply, and to strengthen his faith."[53] In Milne's journal of 1817, he confirmed that Liang and another baptized Chinese, Cai Gao (or Tsae A-ko, [1788–1818]), were "sincere, tho[ugh] very imperfect, Christians."[54] In the same

---

49. Smither, *Augustine as Mentor*, 12–13.

50. Smither, *Augustine as Mentor*, 13–23, 22.

51. Morrison, *Memoirs*, 2:161; McNeur, *China's First Preacher*, 39.

52. Originally, McNeur quoted from the King James Version translation, that is "no longer a servant, but more than a servant, a brother beloved." A modern translation, English Standard Version, has been used instead. McNeur, *China's First Preacher*, 29.

53. Philip, *Life and Opinion*, 227.

54. William Milne to LMS Directors, Malacca, June 22, 1817; Su, "First

The Mentorship of Liang Fa

journal entry, Milne explained his discipleship of Liang and Cai, which was performed through private meetings in conversation, prayers, Scripture explanation, and encouragement to daily Scripture reading.[55] As Liang continued attending worship services (including communion services), prayer meetings, private Bible study, reading Scripture (the New Testament and few books of the Old Testament), and printing Milne's Chinese tracts, God worked through these means in Liang's heart. On October 16, 1818, Milne wrote in his journal, "at night *Afâh* [Liang Fa] said he wished to devote himself to learning, with a view to promote the Gospel."[56]

In light of Smither's eight characteristics of mentorship, the following section considers Milne's mentorship of Liang in detail. First, mentorship takes place in the context of a group of disciples. After Liang's baptism, he was mentored in the church. For Liang, he was not the only Chinese convert in the Malacca mission station, since Cai Gao was baptized by Morrison on July 16, 1814, which was two years prior to Liang's baptism. In 1817, Milne sought to disciple Liang and Cai together through holding private conversations and prayers, but as Morrison wrote, Cai is "not so docile as [he] could wish."[57] Within half a year, Cai left Malacca and went back to China. This did not stop Milne having meetings with Liang, rather Milne met with Liang more on a regular basis for prayer meetings (eight o'clock every Tuesday evening), and for Bible studies (four o'clock every Monday, Wednesday, Thursday and Friday afternoon).[58] For Liang, it was in a church context that he was being discipled and mentored by Milne. In 1819, Liang left

---

Protestant Convert of China," 241.

55. LMS/UG/MA/ 01/02/B; Su, "First Protestant Convert of China," 241.

56. Morrison, *Memoirs*, 50.

57. Robert Morrison to G. Burder, Canton, January 1, 1816; Morrison, *Memoirs*, 1:439; Su, "First Protestant Convert of China," 239.

58. On October 19, 1818, Milne wrote in his journal, "this evening Meng-Ko [another hired printer] intimated a wish to become a Christian" (Morrison, *Memoirs*, 51). The next day, Milne met Liang Fa and Meng-Ko together in the evening. Later in Milne's journal, there is no more mention about meeting with Meng-Ko, and Milne's meetings with Liang were scheduled regularly. Morrison, *Memoirs*, 89–90; Su, *Open Up, China!*, 145.

Training Laborers for His Harvest

Milne and went back to China seeking to be married, and a year later, after experiencing persecution of the Chinese government, he came back to Malacca. In 1820, Liang was put in the newly established Anglo-Chinese College (1818), where Milne was the first principal, and Liang received theological education. In a college report Morrison wrote, "Leang A Fah, Cantonese, aged 35, January 1820 to May 1821; made good progress in theological studies, partly on the funds."[59] In 1821, Liang went back to China to see his newborn son, and after some discussion with his wife, Liang again left his wife, and now a son, behind and came back to Malacca. Liang was "welcomed as a brother by Dr. Milne, and it was arranged that he should give most of his time to study of the Bible."[60] Milne's health declined and he soon died of lung disease on June 2, 1822, and this mentorship ended. On November 20, 1823, Liang brought his son to be baptized by Morrison at Canton, where Liang studied under him for about one month, until Morrison went back to England on December 5 aboard the EIC's *Waterloo* (he arrived on March 20, 1824).[61] Before Morrison's departure, he ordained Liang as the first Chinese Protestant pastor.[62]

Second, the mentor is still a disciple, which means, "though far from having 'arrived' spiritually, the mentor was still growing,

---

59. Morrison, *To the Public*, 6; Harrison, *Waiting for China*, 129.

60. McNeur, *China's First Preacher*, 37.

61. Morrison, *Memoirs*, 2:235, 236.

62. In a letter Milne wrote to Morrison on November 3, 1820, Milne suggested that Morrison might ordain Liang. Milne wrote, "Should Afâh [Liang Fa] continue steady in his profession, and in the pursuit of knowledge, and in his desire for usefulness, for a year or two longer, would it be advisable to ordain him before his return to China, that he might be qualified to administer Christian ordinances in case of your death, or in case of any converts being obtained who could not come to you for baptism?" Morrison, *Memoirs*, 2:73. Concerning the year of Liang's ordination, Robert Philip made a mistake, since he wrote in his *Life and Opinion*, "still farther to qualify himself to preach the Gospel, A-Fa continued his studies with Dr. Morrison for about two or three years [which means from 1822–1824/1825], who then, having sufficient evidence of his qualification for an evangelist, 'laid hands on me, and ordained me he says, 'to publish to men every where the true Gospel'" (Philip, *Life and Opinion*, 231). This contradicts to Morrison's journal about his departure which was in December 1823.

The Mentorship of Liang Fa

his conduct becoming more and more Christlike," which "demonstrated authenticity and humility for [the mentor's] disciples, making his mentoring more attractive and effective."[63] Spiritually, Milne depended on God throughout his ministry, which is reflected in his journal (especially his prayers in the beginning of every new year). On January 1, 1818, Milne concluded his retrospection by praying:

> In thy sight, O God! and in the presence of my brethren, I feel my sinfulness and unfruitfulness—yet desire to raise my Ebenezer [1Sam 7:12, meaning "stone of help"] to thy goodness—"Hitherto hath the Lord helped."[64]

When facing criticism and slander from within the newly established Ultra-Ganges Mission, particularly from Claudius Henry Thomsen and Walter Henry Medhurst in 1819, Milne prayed: ". . . let me learn never to take men at their worst. Help me, Lord! and if any of these charges are just, graciously pardon—for who shall stand if thou, O Lord, shouldst mark iniquity."[65] On February 7, 1819, after testing Liang on expositing John 3:16, Milne blamed himself for Liang's mistakes: "how difficult it is to explain the doctrine of redemption to the heathen mind, so as to convey, I will not say an adequate, but a just view of the subject."[66] In Rachel's sickness, Milne prayed, "Trouble comes thick upon me—O for patience, self-command, prayerfulness of spirit, and grace, both

---

63. Smither, *Augustine as Mentor*, 15, 16.

64. Morrison, *Memoirs*, 49.

65. Milne wrote on January 6, 1819, describing his situation since January 4: "these three days I have had a dreadful onset . . ., and a great deal of personal abuse and impertinent language poured upon on me, and, as I conceive, very unjustly and ungratefully. I have tried to bear it. O that my efforts to bear this load may not be the bare effect of a natural temper, or of calculating discretion; but of a divine principle. . . It has been partly said in words, and partly insinuated, that I am a deceiver—an imposter—a deluder of the public—a Pope—insincere—careless—imprudent; and insinuations of my ignorance of men, imperiousness, want of humility, &c. have been thrown out." Morrison, *Memoirs*, 56.

66. Ibid., 57.

to her and myself, to make a right use of this affliction."[67] In and after Rachel's death, Milne exemplified to Liang a Christian lover, husband, and father in his learning to live as a widower. In regards to Rachel Milne's influence on Liang, McNeur specifies that it was Rachel who "had taught [Liang] what a Christian home could be."[68] Undoubtedly, with having regular prayer meetings with Milne, Liang would learn Milne's struggles, and his personal hope in God.

Third, the mentor selects disciples to join in spiritual growth and serving the community. Though it was Liang who first asked to be trained to be an evangelist, since Liang's baptism Milne had hoped that Liang would witness to other Chinese. For Milne, "to make men well acquainted with the word of God, . . . [is the only way] they can be really useful in turning other sinners to God and holiness."[69] As Milne tested and evaluated Liang, Milne invited Liang to help him to edit the mission's Chinese magazine, *Chinese Monthly Magazine* (察世俗每月統記傳1815–1821). According to the personal weekly schedule that Milne reported to the LMS, he was busy with responsibilities in pastorate, editing, teaching, and evangelizing. Yet, Milne was willing to spend time twice a week with Liang, which displays the special attention Milne paid to Liang's spiritual growth and theological education.

Fourth, the mentorship is a caring personal relationship, which "characterized by both discipline and grace."[70] Milne described Liang as one "of a steady character, and frugal habits. His temper is not so sociable and engaging as that of many other Chinese. He was formerly stiff and obstinate, and occasionally troublesome."[71] Milne patiently and kindly awaited the work of regeneration in Liang's life, and was gladdened by his change. When Liang was tested and failed in explaining Christ's atonement, Milne did not give up on Liang. By correcting Liang, Milne also realized the importance of clarification, and the need of catechism

---

67. Ibid., 58.
68. McNeur, *China's First Preacher*, 31.
69. Philip, *Life and Opinion*, 228.
70. Smither, *Augustine as Mentor*, 17.
71. Philip, *Life and Opinion*, 225.

The Mentorship of Liang Fa

for Liang.[72] In April 1819, when Liang left Milne, Milne wrote in his journal: "A-fâh, the Chinese Christian, left us.—After giving him some suitable instruction—after prayer and many tears, we parted.—The Lord keep him steady and faithful unto death."[73] In a letter he wrote to Morrison concerning Liang's second departure in 1820, Milne expressed his unwillingness to part with him: "he [Liang] talks of returning next summer [1821], but I hope he may be persuaded to remain a little longer."[74] For Milne, though Liang at first was his hired employee, at this point, their relationship to his employer had changed as Philemon's once had to Paul.

Fifth, as Smither wrote, "a hallmark of the Christian movement, provided a point of reference not only for teaching sound doctrine but also for guarding against unsound teaching."[75] From the beginning of Milne's mentorship of Liang, Milne highly elevated the Scriptures as essentially central to Christian life, as Milne believed that it is only by acquainting men with the Scriptures that "the regeneration and sanctification of their own souls can be effected."[76] By having such conviction in mind, Milne would read the Scriptures with Liang once a week with explanation for Liang's edification. In testing Liang, Milne learned that "he wrote very good sense, but left out the article of redemption; and, expecting the divinity of Christ, made it exactly a Socinian discourse on the design of Christ's coming into the world."[77] Milne corrected Liang, and sought solutions to prevent further theological misunderstanding that Liang may have. As has been argued previously in last chapter, Milne's theological root is Jonathan Edwards, and as a result, the theological framework Liang received was Calvinistic.

Sixth, the mentor ought to model a faithful example in work and ministry, involve the disciple in practice in ministry, and

---

72. Morrison, *Memoirs*, 57–58.
73. Ibid., 69.
74. Morrison, *Memoirs*, 2:73.
75. Smither, *Augustine as Mentor*, 19.
76. Philip, *Life and Opinion*, 228.
77. Morrison, *Memoirs*, 57.

debrief "successes and failures in preparation for future ministry."[78] Milne came to China in 1813 and left works unfinished when he died in 1822. Liang was with Milne from the beginning of his ministry in China, and for nine years, Liang met and had a faithful example in Milne, who for the sake of the glory of God and the lost souls in China left his country and spent his energy and life on works, which man's hands cannot accomplish. As McNeur wrote, "[Milne] left a wonderful record of unremitting toil, saintliness of life, and high attainment, but the greatest work Dr. Milne had done . . . was the winning and training of his Chinese brother Liang A-fa."[79] It could be imagined that Milne would be glad to hear Liang preach the gospel in his own tongue to his people, yet Milne was not able to involve Liang much more in ministry than guiding and helping him in the writing and publishing of gospel tracts.

Seventh, the mentor should release the disciple in ministry by increasing his involvement and responsibility. Though Milne never found the opportunity for Liang to take more responsibility in ministry, from Milne's journal and letter, Milne was inclined towards releasing Liang for further ministry. On April 22, 1821, Milne wrote in his journal concerning Liang's second return to China:

> A-Fâh preparing to return to China again. O that his return may be the means of good to our cause --the means of spreading the gospel—and of bringing souls ultimately to Christ;—and tend to open a door of faith to his countrymen. Spent some time in conversation and prayer with him.[80]

From the text itself, Milne expressed his hope that Liang would commit to the Great Commission personally among his countrymen by witnessing Christ in words and in walk. Yet in the context of Milne's suggestion to ordain Liang when wrote to Morrison in November 1820, this text should be understood as

78. Smither, *Augustine as Mentor*, 22.
79. McNeur, *China's First Preacher*, 38.
80. Morrison, *Memoirs*, 99.

The Mentorship of Liang Fa

if Milne would send Liang into a mission field Milne could not reach.[81]

Eighth, the mentor is also "a resource or consultant" to the disciple, who would offer encouragement and practical advices. As it can be found in Milne's mentorship of Liang, conversion is the beginning of discipleship. For Milne, it is essential to contextualize English worship and resources in understandable Chinese without losing its gospel content. The translation of the Scriptures was the major task of Morrison and Milne. Based on Milne's own spiritual growth, he understood the importance of utilizing various means, such as books, for personal spirituality. On December 13, 1818, Milne wrote in his journal, that the church "began singing in Chinese. We have now prayer, reading, preaching, and singing; and have dispensed Baptism and the Lord's Supper in Chinese."[82] As Liang found the need of biblical commentaries, Milne planned to translate commentaries for helping converts like Liang to understand the Scriptures. Milne finished a commentary on the book of Ephesians, which was not published until 1825.[83] As the first principal of the Anglo-Chinese College, Milne understood the importance of theological references, and had deliberately collected books of various languages from donations in order to enlarge the college's library.[84]

CONCLUSION

From the analysis above, it is evident that William Milne's purpose in mentoring Liang Fa was for the winning of his soul; yet it

---

81. Ibid., 2:73.

82. Morrison, *Memoirs*, 51–52.

83. Wylie wrote about this book in his *Memorials*: "Commentary on Ephesians. 104 leaves. Malacca, 1825. From the running title of this volume, it would appear that Dr. Milne merely intended this as an instal[l]ment towards a Commentary on the New Testament. There is a prefatory introduction of ten leaves." Wylie, *Memorials*, 19.

84. A list of books that had been donated to the Anglo-Chinese College can be found in *The Indo-Chinese Gleaner* 6 (October 1818): 213–15.

was more,--he discipled Liang to be an able witness for his Lord among his own people. Nevertheless, Milne understood that, "man may make a preacher, but God only can make a minister."[85] For Milne, gospel-ministry was "only considered as a mean of salvation," by which it is the Holy Spirit who works in the heart of men, like Liang Fa.[86] Compared with the previous attempts of the Nestorians and the Roman Catholics, who failed to plant the gospel seed in the soil of China, Milne mentored men like Liang to read, understand, and preach the Scriptures with a sound Christ-centered theological framework. Robert Morrison and William Milne depended on the Lord of the harvest alone in their ministry, which enabled them to "expect great things from God, and attempt great things for God" in practice in China, while William Carey, William Ward (1769–1823) and Joshua Marshman (1768–1837) worked in India for the same harvest.[87]

---

85. Cowie, *Dissenter's Guide*, 8.
86. Ibid., 7.
87. Bebbington, *Baptists*, 218.

Conclusion

THE HISTORIAN'S BUSINESS, AS defined by James M. Banner, Jr., is to be one who seeks "to know what happened in the past and why it did so and then to present that knowledge to others in the formats . . . of their choice."[1] Yet, as David Bebbington argues, historians are limited by the problems of "the evidence" and "of the historian himself."[2] He further argues that the historian's writing is "the result of an interaction between the givenness of the past and the creativeness of the historian [based on the historian's values, outlook and worldview]."[3] Thus, a historian "characteristically argues [and presents] reasons for adopting a particular version of the past," a process in which rhetoric--the art of persuasion--is employed.[4] Christian historians understand history with three convictions drawn out of biblical truth, which are "God intervenes in [history]," "[God] guides [history] in a straight line," and "[God] will bring [history] to the conclusion that he has planned."[5] Moreover, for Augustine, "the whole of human history was articulated in terms of decisive landmarks within the history of salvation."[6] Since God reveals himself to humanity through the inspiration of the Bible, and "all historical events are subject

1. Banner, *Being a Historian*, 3-4.
2. Bebbington, *Patterns in History*, 5.
3. Ibid., 12.
4. Ibid., 14.
5. Ibid., 43.
6. Markus, "History," 433. Also see Löwith, *Meaning in History*, 160-73.

to his overruling omnipotence and inescapable serve his intended ends," Carl F. H. Henry is correct to argue that "divine revelation is the epistemic source and Scripture the methodological principle of the Christian interpretation of history."[7] With this kind of Christocentric worldview, this book has purposefully examined the life and mission of the early Protestant missionaries in China, particularly in regard to William Milne's mentorship of Liang Fa. By collecting historical facts, this book has reconstructed the historical setting and theological framework of the Ultra-Ganges missionaries, like Robert Morrison, William Milne and Liang Fa. In other words, Morrison and Milne's missionary works are examined by being relocated in the larger context of the redemptive history. Hence this study is not hagiographical; rather, it is a historical interpretation of David Bogue's statement:

> People consider missionaries going forth among the heathen as mere men, with no wisdom superior to their own, with no strength above human, and they are greatly dispirited; but did we view a missionary as we ought, and as he is, with Jesus his Master at his right-hand, accompanying him on the way, and the Holy Spirit resting on him like a flame of fire, with all his powerful energies, we could not be cast down, but maintain a cheerful hope amidst the darkness appearances of Pagan ignorance and obstinacy, and persevere, trusting in the Lord, and in the power of his might.[8]

Such a statement restores the glory of the sovereign God of history, and testifies that "for those who love God all things work together for good, for those who are called according to his purpose" (Rom 8:28). It also matches Milne's understanding of the gospel mission with his spirituality as reflected in his prayers. It is certain that archival research is essential for study like this, but it is also undeniable that facts need to be arranged and analyzed within the worldview of those who made and engaged in those facts.

---

7. Henry, *God, Revelation and Authority*, 2:254, 320.
8. Bogue, *Objections*, 15.

Conclusion

In contrast to the conclusions of most contemporary scholars, this book demonstrated that the primary goal of Robert Morrison and William Milne's mission was to make Christian converts among the Chinese.[9] Moreover, Morrison and Milne also followed the Edwardsean root they had inherited from Bogue, to plant Chinese churches characterized by their self-supporting, self-governing, and self-propagating nature. In the historical and social context of the Qing dynasty, the spiritual quality and maturity of a Chinese convert was far more important than the quantity of converts. Though in Milne's life, he only baptized two converts (Liang Fa on November 3, 1816, and a woman called Johanna on July 1, 1821), which seems to be little fruit compared to later missionaries like J. Hudson Taylor (1832–1905), God prospered Milne's mentorship of Liang Fa, as Milne prayed, in making the gospel take root in China.

Many scholars today are attracted to the political and cultural impact of Taiping Rebellion (December 1850–August 1864) led by Hong Xiuquan (洪秀全, 1814–1864), which was influenced and inspired by Liang Fa's *Good Words Exhorting the Age* (勸世良言).[10] Yet, behind Hong's Taiping Heavenly Kingdom there was a religious conviction, an eschatological agenda––to establish the heavenly kingdom on earth, in replacement of the Manchurian Qing dynasty.[11] Theologically, Hong Xiuquan and his Taiping Heavenly

---

9. Scholars like Odd Arne Westad doubted and denied Morrison and Milne's primary goal of mission. In his book *Restless Empire*, Westad wrote, "China's encounter with Christianity from the sixteenth century on had primarily happened through European Catholics, but most of the nineteenth-century missionaries were British or American Protestants. They were young men and women inspired by the Great Awakening in the United States and evangelical revivals in Britain. Some of the most influential of these missionaries were interested more in propagating Western educational ideals than in saving souls." Westad, *Restless Empire*, 70.

10. Chinese communist politician Mao Zedong praised the achievement of the Taiping Rebellion as foreshadowing the communist revolution (Mao, *Collected Writings*, 116–17, 125–26, 152.). Other contemporary political and cultural studies of the Taiping Rebellion see Spence, *God's Chinese Son*; Platt, *Autumn in the Heavenly Kingdom*; and Kuhn, *Rebellion and Its Enemies*.

11. On the religious root of Taiping Rebellion see Foster, "Christian

Kingdom movement is a form of syncretism, and therefore a heresy to the Christian church. However, the Taiping Rebellion in its religious nature reflected the fact that the Chinese intellectuals then considered Christianity to be a third philosophical option in addition to the established Confucianism and Buddhism in imperial China. The Nestorians and the Roman Catholics were not able to achieve this. As this book tries to demonstrate, it was through William Milne's mentorship of Liang Fa, that such intellectual influence was achieved. A gospel foundation had been established in China, from which the future missionaries were able to reap a vast harvest in the mission field of China.

As Christopher A. Daily has rightfully argued, a study like this needs to be complemented by further archival discoveries in order to support its argument more sufficiently.[12] Yet, this book provides reflections for contemporary churches both in China and overseas. First, in the practice of contextualization, the gospel must be faithfully presented to people in their cultural context, in order to help them clearly understand the gospel. Second, this book helps the Chinese church to rediscover its theological heritage, which is Edwardsean Calvinism, from Bogue, through Morrison and Milne. Third, it is hoped that the study in this book will help the church and missionary organizations to rediscover the biblical missiological methods practiced by Paul the apostle, especially in the mentorship of disciples and future leaders.

Origins," 156–67; Bohr, "Heavenly Kingdom in China," 38–52; Wheeler, "Chinese Hussites," 223–24; Wagner, *Reenacting the Heavenly Vision*.

12. Daily, *Robert Morrison*, 198–202.

Appendix 1
Regulations Governing Foreign Trade Up To 1840[1]

1. No foreign warships may sail inside the Bogue (the harbor approach to Canton city);
2. Neither foreign women nor firearms may be brought into the factories (the warehouse complex reserved for foreign traders within the harbor but outside Canton city walls);
3. . . . foreign ships must not enter into direct communication with the Chinese people and merchants without the immediate supervision (of a native Chinese);
4. Each factory (each trading nation had its own "factory") is restricted for its service to 8 Chinese (irrespective of the number of its occupants) . . .
5. Foreigners may not communicate with Chinese officials expect through the proper channel of the Co-hong (i.e., appointees from among the native Chinese merchants at Canton);
6. Foreigners are not allowed to row boats freely in the river . . . On the 8th, 18th, and 28th days of the moon "they may take the air . . . All ships' boats passing the Custom-house on the river must be detained and examined, to guard against guns, swords, or firearms being furtively carried in them. On the

---

1. Adopted from Hsu, *Rise of Modern China*, 21.

Appendix 1

8th, 18th, and 28th days of the moon these foreign barbarians may visit the Flower Gardens and the Honam Joss-house, but not in droves of over ten at one time . . . If the ten should presume to enter villages, public places, or bazaars, punishment will be inflicted upon the (interpreter) who accompanies them;

7. Foreign trade must be conducted through the Hong merchants. Foreigners living in the factories must not move in and out too frequently, although they may walk freely within a hundred yards of their factories . . .

8. Foreign traders must not remain Canton after the trading season (which lasted from October to May each year) . . . they should return home or go to Macao (the Portuguese enclave at the mouth of the harbor);

9. Foreigners may neither buy a Chinese book, nor learn Chinese . . .

10. The Hong merchants shall not go into debt to foreigners.

Appendix 2

To Pious Men[1]

My dear Christian Friends,

Hundreds of millions of Pagans are perishing for lack of the knowledge of God, and of Jesus Christ his Son, whom to know is everlasting life. The London Missionary Society wants Missionaries to go and turn them from darkness to light, and from the power of Satan unto God. As a member of the Society, I say in their name, we expected, at its first institution, that multitudes would have offered themselves for the glorious service. The flourishing state of religion throughout the country, and the vast numbers of young disciples who crowded the places of worship, impressed us with the idea that restrained would be necessary, not repeated calls for labourers in the harvest. But, ah! how much were we mistaken! It is now the tenth year of our institution, and we want Missionaries, and have long wanted them, for the vast fields which open to us on every side.

    To that honour, ye Pious Youths of Britain, are ye called! Many of us, who have numbered more than fifty years, lament that, in our younger days, no such prospects appeared before our eyes; but though to us it was denied to plant the Standard of the Cross in Heathen lands, the envied honour is reserved for you. And will ye not grasp at it with eagerness, and say, "Lord, here am I, send me?"--'I am willing,' says one, 'but I am afraid that I have

---

1. Anonymous, "To Pious Young Men," 169-71.

not the qualifications requisite.—Whom do you want?' We want young men who have tasted that the Lord is gracious, and have been renewed in the spirit of their minds:—we want young men of good abilities, and capable of improvement; and if they have been improved by literature, so much the better: --we want young men whose conduct during the course of their religious profession has manifested stability, purity, and prudence:—we want young men burning with zeal for the salvation of immortal souls, and panting for the propagation of the gospel among the Heathen. It is you that we want. You who are thus endowed, come forward to the service.

Ministers and private Christians of a public spirit, give us your aid. Mark such youths, recommend the service of the Heathen to their serious regard; bring them forward and present them to us; say not, "We need such young men at home, and cannot spare them." Send them, and God will raise you up more. If you will keep them at home, God, by way of punishment, may make them pricks in your eyes, and thorns in your sides.

Students in academies, with particular earnestness we invite you to devote yourselves to Missionary labours. To be an apostle of a Pagan nation, how much more glorious than to be the minister of a congregation of a few hundred people in England! To preach Christ's gospel where his name was never heard before, how much more honourable and delightful, than to go to an old cultivated field, where the Redeemer's names has sounded for ages, and where a preacher could easily be found!

Tutors and Managers of Academies we entreat; nay, as pleading the cause of Christ and of the Heathen, we demand your aid. But we need not. We are confident we have you on our side. There cannot be, at the present time, the tutor of an evangelical academy who would not rejoice at seeing the students offer themselves for the Missionary service, and who would not account it a duty of no common magnitude, to animate them to the work.

Some pious young men are saying, while they read, "With pleasure would I accept your invitation; but I am afraid that I am not called; and to run unsent, is a dreadful thing!" Hear me, my dear friends. With respect to your abilities, others can judge more properly than yourselves. A minister, zealous for the propagation of the gospel; a judicious Christian of enlarged views; or, in default of both, a Director of the Missionary Society, to whom you can easily be introduced, will be a proper person to decide the matter. But as to a call, as it respects the qualifications of the heart, we ask, Do you feel yourselves entirely devoted to the service of the Redeemer? Is it your desire to spend your days in preaching the gospel to the Heathen? Is it a steady, fixed, abiding, increasing desire? Is it a desire which at once humbles you into the dust as nothing, and draws you with the cords of love to Missionary work? If so, be not uneasy about you call. He who hath wrought these dispositions in you is God, who also hath given unto you his Holy Spirit. In this way does the apostle Paul state the subject: "If any man desire the office of a bishop, he desireth a good work." He places the call in the desire, and immediately proceeds to the qualifications.

"But I am not qualified," I hear a youth object; "and the work is arduous." You may not be qualified to be a Missionary at the present time; but you may be qualified to enter on a course of preparatory studies for the work of a Missionary. Peter, Andrew, James, and John, when they left their boats on the sea of Galilee, were not fit to go forth as apostles to convert the nations to the faith; but they were fit to go as students into the seminary of Jesus Christ. "But the work is arduous." It is preaching the gospel; and the man who understands the gospel so well as to be able to preach it, when he has once inquired the language of the Heathen, need not doubt of divine assistance and success; for the gospel is the power of God unto salvation!

Does some one say, "I have applied to my minister, and to Christian friends; but they discourage me from the attempt?" Is your minister's breast burning with zeal for the conversion of the Heathen? Do his prayers, does his preaching, does his conversation display the ardour of a soul inflamed with affection for the perishing Pagans? If so, there is reason to pause:—if not, why should you expect that he will give you encouragement in a work, in respect to which he himself is destitute of zeal? Apply to another quarter.

Appendix 2

Lift up your eyes, my young friends, and behold the fields of labour into which we call you to work. There is a beautiful variety suited to every taste. He who considers himself as best adapted for the rude sons of uncultivated life, will find a people to his wish in Southern Africa. To die youth, who prefers a state of high civilization, India and China stretch out their hands. Should a state of society between these two be more congenial to another, to such a country he will be sent.

Wealth we cannot promise as your reward. Like your Master, you will be poor. Worldly honours and dignities we have not to bestow; you may be despised and reproached for your work's sake. Earthly pleasures are not to be expected;—you may be called to suffer for the cause of Christ. But we can promise you the affection and esteem of brethren and friends;—we can promise you the prayers of the ten thousands of spiritual Israel;—we can promise you the presence of the great Head of the Church;—we can promise you that peace in his service which the world cannot give, and which the world cannot take away;—and we can assure you, that every Missionary who is faithful unto death, shall receive a crown of glory, which fadeth not away.

Another Annual Meeting of the Society is at hand: attend it; and there offer yourselves to be Missionaries of Christ, to carry his name far hence unto the Heathen!

—A Friend of Missions

Appendix 3
Memoir of Mrs. Milne[1]

RACHEL, THE WIFE OF the Rev. W[illiam] Milne, Malacca, who died on the 20th March, 1819, was born of respectable parents, in the city of Aberdeen, North of Scotland, on the 23rd September, 1783. Her father Charles Cowie, Esq. was extensively engaged as a stocking manufacturer and hosier, in which line of business he was enabled to support a large family in comfortable circumstances, and give them an education suited to their rank in society. But change of times and the failure of foreign commerce, threw him ultimately into great difficulties, the pressure of which would have been insupportable, but for the filial piety, diligence, and prudence, of his youngest daughter, *Rachel*, the subject of this paper.

From her earliest infancy, Rachel's parents endeavoured to impress religious truth upon her mind. In her diary she gives this honorable testimony to her mother's conduct: "My mother's instructions were enforced by her prayers and example." Her parents were originally members of the Church of Scotland, but in consequence of the removal of their Minister, the family joined the Congregational Church, now under the care of the Rev. John Philip, Aberdeen. When about the eighth year of her age, Rachel was at times seriously impressed with a sense of the omniscience of God; but often felt evil and blasphemous thoughts rising up in the mind, which proved a great source of uneasiness and deep

---

1. Milne, "Memoir of Mrs. Milne," 103–15.

self-abasement. She prayed earnestly to God, and was delivered from them. But soon forgot her obligations to divine goodness. In Scotland, the female members of many families, in the higher ranks of society, as well as of those in middling circumstances, are instructed in some branch of business, suited to the strength and station of the sex. This practice cannot be sufficiently applauded. Much domestic virtue and comfort arrive from it. The knowledge of it is easily carried about with them; and should they ever stand in need of having recourse to it for personal support, or for the comport of aged parents, it may enable them to procure necessaries, comforts, and abundance; and to preserve that independence of spirit which should be cherished in every community, and which strongly characterizes the people of Scotland.

Rachel was early put to learn a branch of the millinery business. The circumstances of the family at that time rendered it unnecessary to attend to that as a means of support; but in the course of those revolutions which were awaiting her, and her parents in the dispensations of providence, it proved of the greatest service. But while acquiring a knowledge of this, and attending to other ornamental branches of education, she was led into the society of those whose conversation and manners were calculated to weaken the force of parental instruction; and to produce a vitiated taste for the gayety and pleasures of the world. The reading of novels—dancing, of which she was enthusiastically fond—the ball room—gay company—and the public amusements,—soon engrossed her thoughts, and tended to create a distaste for the nobler enjoyments of religion, and the more rational pursuits of life. These are I doubt not, their general effects in society, however unwilling persons may be acknowledge it.

But God was pleased to water by the influence of his grace, the seeds of instruction sown by the parental hand. Former impressions were received and deepened, under the preaching of the Gospel. Such had been the influence of public amusements, and of the conversion of ungodly persons on Rachel's mind, that she went one sabbath afternoon in company with a few thoughtless companions to Church to see what materials for light remark and

Memoir of Mrs. Milne

laughter they could collect from the preacher's sermon and manner. The Rev. James Bennet[t (1774–1862)], now Theological Tutor at Rotherham Academy, was to preach. The eloquent address of that popular and useful Minister, deeply arrested her attention; and those who went to laugh, remained to hear. The importance of the truths delivered, fell with weight on Rachel's heart. She henceforth attended the ordinances of the sabbath with increased seriousness and delight; and all the more private means of social worship and Christian edification. She had always indeed attended public worship, and was never so far left as to run into the common vices of youth; or entirely to cast off a sense of religion; but now it became the serious concern of the mind, and the business of life. Her own sinfulness and the necessity of a Redeemer were discovered; and she was *to give herself up to God*, and by faith to commit her immortal interests to Jesus Christ as her all-sufficient Saviour. The labors of the Rev. Mr. Stevens, she often mentioned with high satisfaction, as having derived great benefit from them.

Rachel was by this time grown up—and her fond parents thought it necessary that she should see a little more of life. She accordingly visited London and spent some time there. She was introduced into the society of persons of distinction; and visited the chief places of public resort and curiosity. The novel scenes of the splendid metropolis, she felt had a tendency to dissipate the mind, to unfit it for the duties of the closet, and the sober concerns of life.

While in London, she attended the anniversary of the Missionary Society, the services of which produced so deep an impression of the importance of sending the gospel to the heathen, that she lamented that the circumstance of her sex prevented her from taking any part therein. This idea, romantic as it may appear to some, was probably the commencement of that train of events, which ultimately induced her to prefer the company of one who was destined to labor among the heathen, before that of others in conne[ct]ion with whom she might have had the prospects of ease, independence, and wealth at home; although it was six years afterwards before she had any opportunity of forming a decision

Appendix 3

on this head. To such apparently little circumstances, do the events of human life frequently owe their beginnings.

She was shortly after her return from London, received as a member of the Church, and sat down at the Lord's [T]able, to commemorate the sufferings and death of Jesus. Through the whole of her future life, she always attended this ordinance with peculiar delight, generally found it edifying, and wished more frequent returns of the opportunity of celebrating it.

The stated dispensation of gospel ordinances, after the settlement of the Rev. John Philip [1775–1851], in Aberdeen, through the divine blessing, increased her knowledge of the Scriptures, and strengthened her resolutions to serve and glorify God; while in the daily morning and evening worship of her father's family, she derived the most solid advantages for edification. Happy are the children of those who fear God!—[A]nd happy are those Christians, who live in families where God is statedly, and reverently worshipped!

The time now approached when Rachel's trials were to begin. Her mother, through accumulated infirmities, was frequently unable to leave her chamber. For some time, her father's business had been on the decline, and an entire stop being put by the war, to all commercial intercourse with Holland, France, and other parts of the Continent, on which the success of his business chiefly depended, the House could consequence, no longer pay its bills, and became insolvent. To Rachel this was a source of unspeakable anxiety. Her only surviving brother, scarcely out from school, could not well do for himself. Her sister with a young family, could render no assistance. Her parents now both infirm, and greatly harassed by inconsiderable and unmerciful requisitions, had no means of supporting of their old age. A conscientious with to discharge the demands of their creditors as far as possible, led them to give up every thing, except their wearing apparel and a few books.

It was in these circumstances that the filial affection of Rachel shone forth conspicuously. It had ever been their aim, in the course of her education, to form in her mind rational and sober views of life, and to fix her attention most on those acquirements which are most useful—which endure the test of affliction; and which wear to the last hour of life; and they were themselves among the first to reap the advantages. Rachel, seeing the declining state of her father's business, thought it her duty before hand, to make some preparation for future exigencies. She accordingly, with the consent of her parents, began business in the millinery line; partly with a view to ease them of the expense of her support and partly with a view to provide for them in case of insolvency. She had only a few pounds of money of her own to begin with; but she borrowed a small sum from a friend; and, being conscious that her motives were upright and honorable, she earnestly prayed that God would prosper the work of her hands, and preserve her from the snares to which this new situation would expose her. Her efforts were so far crowned with success, that in a few months she was able to repay what she had borrowed, to furnish a house comfortably, and to leave something over. She now took her destitute parents both to her own house; supported them by her labors; nursed them with the utmost tenderness in their afflictions; attended them in their last moments; saw them die in hope of the glory of God; and interred their mortal remains with decency and respect.

She had ever been their favorite child; but who can tell the feelings of the aged and dying parents, when nursed and attended day and night by such a daughter, in whose countenance the most cheerful satisfaction with her lot, the most anxious wish to serve them, and the most painful solicitude to render the pains of death easier, were ever pointed? Ten thousands of blessings from haven were daily implored to rest upon her head; and the expiring parents both expressed to her a hope, that "God would make all her bed in her sickness;" and raise up kind and tender-hearted friends to her in every extremity--which hope was actually realized in course of her future life. For, in the many personal and domestic afflictions which she had afterwards to pass through, the hand of God, in raising up kind friends where no obligations existed, and in providing medical attendants, who acted as fathers and brothers to her,—was peculiarly visible. It was remarked both by herself and her husband. It is worthy of being recorded as an encouragement

Appendix 3

to filial piety, and as a proof that the prayers of pious parents are available with God, for blessings on dutiful children. Reader, learn and imitate.—In her diary, she has taken notice of the gracious Providence of God in providing for her and her parents in their afflictions, and concludes by remarking: "I have enlarged more on this part of my narrative than I at first intended, because it shows the wisdom and goodness of God, and the implicit confidence which his people may place in his promises, that he will supply all their wants; though perhaps not exactly in the way they think or wish."

While her parents stood in need of her assistance, Rachel could never think it right to listen to any proposals of marriage, though many advantageous ones had been made. About twelve months after her mother's death, an acquaintance was formed between her and the person who ultimately became her husband.

What is commonly called the season of courtship, was not passed over by Rachel, as it too frequently is, in cherishing extravagant fancies about "the pure and unmixed bliss of the conjugal state"—or in lavishingly wasting her money on the purchases of finery; no,—but in preparing herself for the discharge of the new and important duties of the relation upon which she was about to enter. She considered the practice of many young persons to domestic life—and indeed, as the presage of much misery. The listless, flippant vanity of multitudes of young ladies, she viewed as highly dishonorable to the sex. She believed that all the events of life are ordered by divine providence, and that the duties of each human relation are binding by a divine sanction. This led her often to her knees to implore the direction of God, and grace to discharge the duties that were awaiting her.

Thus prepared by education, by piety, by the reverses of fortune, by afflictions, by habits of diligence and economy,—she entered into the conjugal state on the 4th August, 1812, the duties of which, as a wife and a mother, she discharged for six years and a half, in such a manner as to reflect the highest honor on her own principles; to make her partner in life the happiest of husbands; to keep her children cleanly in their persons, and neat in their dress;

to preserve the family expense within its resources; to sweeten the cup of domestic affliction, and lighten the burdens of life; to secure the growing affection of those that knew her best; and to draw forth the esteem of neighbours and strangers.

In early life, Mrs. M[ilne] was struck with the description, given by Solomon in the last chapter of the Proverbs, of the "Woman, whose price is above rubies." It was the aim of her parents to make her such as to answer the description; and it was her own constant study to fall as little short of it as possible. Nor is it affirming too much to say, that it would not be easy to find a person who in all respects, comes so near as she did, to the standard of personal, maternal, and domestic worth, fixed by the wise man.

Mrs. Milne had six children, two of whom were called away at an early period. The bereavement, though borne with cordial submission to the divine will, produced a visible damp on her spirits. She never afterwards recovered her natural vivacity. The care of her surviving children, engrossed the chief pat of her solicitude, time, and strength. She powerfully felt the paramount claims of relative duty; and they occupied the first place in her attention, next to the more serious obligations of creatures to their God. She thought very meanly of the religion and understanding of those mothers—who neglected their children, their husbands, and their household affairs.

She loved the word of God; and delighted in the ordinances of divine worship, both in the family and in the church.—In her last illness, she said, "I cannot think favorably of the personal piety of those who neglect family prayer; nor augur much usefulness from those who do not attend on it regularly, when in their power." The salvation of the souls of her children was a subject of her most earnest prayers. The short time she was spared with them, afforded scarce an opportunity of instructing any of them except a little girl, the others being too young to fix their attention. In as far as health would allow, to impart some religious instruction to her daughter, was a work of every day.—She often said—"I have never wished for riches, or fame to our children; but that they may truly fear God, and be good and useful members of society." She had a

Appendix 3

very humbling sense of her own sinfulness, and frequently spoke of herself to her dearest earthly friend, in terms expressive of the deepest self-abasement of soul before God.

Mrs. Milne's heart was much engaged in the good work, to which her husband and herself had devoted their lives. But she had a different idea of the way in which females best subserve the cause of the Gospel among the heathen, from what is entertained by some. She thought that by managing the domestic concerns; by endeavouring to make her husband's mind easy; by a care of his health; by watching to discover those errors which he might overlook; and pointing them out; by assisting him with her counsel; and by such a conduct as would render the mission worthy of respect in the eyes of mankind; in these ways, she conceived Missionary's wife might render no small service to the interests of religion. She was often laying plans for bringing up, and educating a few poor orphan girls; but lived not to see her plans executed. At the Cape of Good Hope, the Isle of France, China, and Malacca, she had many opportunities of witnessing the deplorable condition of those who know not God; she felt and prayed from them; and died in the faith that the labors of Missionaries among the heathen, will in due time be crowned with the richest success.

About two years before her death, Mrs. M[ilne] had a most serious illness, during part of which her life was despaired of both by herself and others. She then made solemn surrender of herself, her husband, and her children, to God her Saviour; and waited the call of death. In the very height of her affliction, the consolations of the Gospel were so abundantly poured into her heart, and her hopes of eternal blessedness so clear, that she afterwards said—"Your intimation that my complaint had taken a favorable turn, filled me with sorrow.—I felt an unspeakable disappointment, to be sent back again as it were from the gates of heaven, to spend a little more time in this sinful and dreary state."—The sublime and consoling truths delivered by our Lord Jesus, previously to his crucifixion, and which are contained in the 14th, 15th, 16th, and 17th chapters of John, afforded inexpressible joy to her soul. She several times said—"the spirit of divine friendship in which they were spoken, independently of their own unspeakable importance, gives a peculiar sweetness to those portions of the New Testament."

By the blessing of God, a voyage to China, and the kind attentions of friends there, (to whom she ever felt grateful) were the means of restoring her to such a measure of health, as that she could attend to the duties of the family; but she never fully recovered her wonted strength. Indeed she sometimes said, that though her life was spared, she conceived it would be but for a short time. This idea seemed to dwell in her mind. She of consequence, spent more time in reading the Scriptures and private devotion than formerly; but never to the neglect of any relative duty.

Dreams and presentiments, though they have both their uses to mankind, are often sources of unspeakable uneasiness to the credulous and weak mankind. We must judge of them as the Israelites were to judge of prophets—that if they thing came to pass they might then be assured the prophet was true, and vice versa. It has been not unfrequently remarked that pious persons shortly before death, have had a kind of presentiment of its approach. This appeared to be the case with Mrs. M[ilne] On the first sabbath of January, about two months and a half previously to her demise, the ordinance of the Lord's Supper was dispensed; and it was a season of peculiar edification to all present: feelings and anticipations of an unusual nature, filled every breast—the tears flowed abundantly from every eye—and the whole seemed as if sent to prepare the way for some important though unforeseen event. Mrs. M[ilne] experienced more than common edification; but in the evening she told some female friends with tears, that "she thought it was very likely the last time she should taste the fruit of the vine with them at the table of the Lord"—and so it proved; for circumstances prevented the celebration of that ordinance again while she was in the body, which she deeply regretted; for she considered this of all Christian ordinances, the most calculated to increase love to the Saviour, and the edification of the soul. On the 6th of February, she was delivered of a son. Her recovery for ten days, went on favorably; and the hoped to be soon able to carry her little one to the House of God, to present him to the Lord in baptism. But she caught cold which was speedily followed by fever, vomiting, and dysentery, which no means could cure. Often expressing an earnest desire solemnly to give up her son to God, he was accordingly baptized at her bedside, after which she felt better satisfied, as having performed an important parental duty. The solemn hour of release from the body, drew near—she became daily weaker. Some flattering intervals of the complaint, encouraged a momentary hope of recovery, which was as frequently disappointed. She spent the moments of ease, in commending her own soul and those of her family to God her Saviour. She enjoyed a steady hope of salvation, but had not those rapturous feelings of joy which she was favored with in a former season of sickness, already alluded to. She often said—"Christ is my only hope; I seek none else,"—and, "I seek not a triumphant death, but a safe and peaceful one."—One morning having been for some time left alone, on her husband's entering the room, she said:—"You have interrupted me—O what a sweet moment I have had!"—She sometimes spoke with the deepest solicitude about her children, especially her little daughter. The idea that she might be left, perhaps fatherless also, in these countries where there is so much to pollute the infant mind, and so few fitted to watch over its gradual buddings and direct it to God,—was quite insupportable; and her mind found relief only by earnest prayer to that God, who is "the orphan's stay."

A change of air was advised, and as there was no opportunity of a sea voyage, a removal to the country was the only alternative left: on the 17th March, she was conveyed to the countryseat of a Gentleman of Malacca. She felt pleased on reaching so retired and peaceful a retreat, where she could enjoy the attentions of her husband; without those interruptions, which were unavoidable in town: she often called him to read some favorite hymns and pray with her. The disease rapidly increased—though she was not conscious of much pain. She several times called her children to see them, and bless them. She felt occasional stupor—was unable to say much—several times expressed that Christ was her only hope. On the 18th, a letter from a particular friend who had shown her

Memoir of Mrs. Milne

much kindness, having come to hand, she was able to hear it read, and the news, together with the association of ideas awakened in the mind thereby, roused her from the stupor induced by the disease; and she spent a few minutes in the attitude of prayer, with her eyes directed towards heaven; imploring no doubt the blessing of God on him and his family. On the 19th, she took leave of several friends who came from town to see her, and blessed them. In course of that night, partial delirium and wanderings were observed; but at intervals the mind was calm and lucid. She said, she felt no pain. Next morning about an hour before her death, a friend went to prayer at her bedside. She was pleased, though scarce able to speak. Her children were brought in to see her for the last time in life; but she was no longer able to speak to them. It was now evident that the time of her departure was at hand. She had latterly experienced a frequent sense of suffocation, occasioned by an astonishing accumulation of phlegm in the throat; and, supposing that this sensation would be peculiarly felt in her last moments, she had, with great calmness of mind before hand, directed her husband to administer some liquids which had often given relief. The constant application of these, seemed to ease the final struggles of expiring life. On the 20th March, (1819,) about nine o'clock in the morning, she was released from the afflictions and infirmities of life. Her eyes were closed in death by the hand of one, who had ever beheld them with delight; and whose only consolation was, that, as he could not enjoy her society any longer on earth, he had good reason to hope, that she was gone to *"be with Christ which is far better."* Mrs. Milne died, aged thirty-five years, five months, and twenty-seven days. Her mortal remains were committed to the dust, in the Dutch Burying Ground, on the following day.

In the close of these brief memoirs, some little circumstances, of not consequence to the general reader, have been noticed for the sake of distant relatives. A few particulars relative to the *character* of the deceased, which could not be so well wrought into the narrative, shall close this paper. Mrs. Milne possessed a peculiar *penetration into the human character*, by a view of the countenance. This is sometimes the case with individuals; and though the decisions thus formed, ought never to assume the authority of a rule to themselves or others; yet providence may have some wise end to answer by giving this talent. The general features of the character—the predominant passions—the chief quality of the temper,—have all been objects of study with the physiognomist. But in the case before us, the discrimination seemed quite natural, without design or effort. She formed a judgment at first sight, and the writer does not recollect a single instance, during upwards of six years, which was not confirmed by facts. Mrs. M[ilne]'s *religion* was drawn from the Scriptures. It sought retirement, was free from ostentation, mixed with no singularities, and was accompanied with deep humility. It was most conspicuous to those who had access to her closet. It was nourished in the shade; and displayed by the discharge of family duties—by sweetness and mildness of temper—by patience under afflictions—by private acts of charity known to few.—Though fit to appear in what is called the best society and fond of social intercourse, Mrs. M[ilne] *loved also to be alone, or busied with her domestic concerns.* She though the mother of a family should feel all her attractions at home—that her children should be her amusement—and the real good of all within the family circle, her constant study. Such were her sentiments, and such was her own conduct. She no [infrequently] expressed her astonishment at the conduct of those ladies to whom their own houses are a sort of prisons—and her utter abhorrence of the conduct of some who "cast aside (as she used to say,) their children as soon as born, to *somebody* to care for them;" who seldom think of them till they be sick or pass recovery through the neglect of servants, or till there be another child to throw aside as the former; and who rather than deny themselves the pleasure of a dance, a ball, or a card party, will leave their afflicted infants under the care of an Indian nurse-maid! It is hoped, that the number of such mothers, (if they deserve that endearing name) in India, is daily diminishing, and that a more serious sense of maternal duty will fill the mind of every Christian female, whatever may be her rank in society.

Memoir of Mrs. Milne

Mrs. M[ilne] had been often in adversity, and hence she became an excellent *sick nurse*. It often fell to her lot to have sick persons to attend upon; and she possessed a degree of tenderness and skill in treating them, which we look for in vain, except from those who possess uncommon kindness of heart, and have been practiced in the school of affliction. To the wives of Missionaries, who may be placed at a distance from medical advice, [knowledge] of the common diseases, at least of children, and the way of treating them, is a very valuable attainment. It may make them useful to their heathen neighbours, as well as to their own families.

After coming to China and Malacca, the duties of the Mission several times called Mrs. M[ilne]'s partner in life to visit other places at a distance. On the occasion of such separations, she endeavoured to moderate her feelings, and, instead of interposing any hindrance, endeavoured to encourage him and to keep up his spirits, hoping that such services would contribute to the promotion of the Saviour's kingdom. She used to say—"However dearly I love your company, I should be sorry to keep you from your duty. I cannot render you much assistance; but I will try not to hinder you: I should be grieved to think that you spent one hour with me, while I am in health, which should be spent in your studies and labours."—Such sentiments were without doubt, founded in a deep conviction of the paramount obligation of *duty*, to every claim which ease or gratification could prefer. Mrs. M[ilne] in her private papers, particularly took notice of two very important eras in the Chinese Mission.—"1. The completion of the New Testament in Chinese.—2. The baptism of the first Chinese convert."— To have seen two things, she thought an ample reward for having left her relatives and country, and come all the way to China. She viewed them as pledges of great future good, and as affording the strongest encouragement to continued diligence and perseverance in the work of the Gospel.

Appendix 4
Works of William Milne[1]

WORKS IN CHINESE

1. A Farewell Address. 3 pages. Batavia, 1814.
2. 求世者言行真史記 Life of Christ. 71 pages. Canton, 1814.
3. 進小門走窄路解論 Tract on the Strait Gate. 10 pages. Malacca, 1816.
4. 崇眞實棄假謊略說 Tract on the Sin of Lying, and the Importance of Truth. 5 pages. Malacca, 1816.
5. 幼學淺解問答 A Catechism for Youth. 37 pages. Malacca, 1817.
6. 祈禱真法註解 Exposition of the Lord's Prayer. 41 pages. Malacca, 1818.
7. 諸國異神論 Tract on Idolatry. 7 pages. Malacca, 1818.
8. 生意公平聚益法 On Justice Between Man and Man. 10 pages. Malacca, 1818.
9. 聖書節註十二訓 Twelve Short Sermons. 12 pages. Malacca, 1818.

1. A catalogue of the works of William Milne was recorded in Wylie, *Memorials*, 12–21. This list of Milne's Chinese and English works are adopted from Wylie's catalogue.

10. 賭博明論略講 The Evils of Gambling. 13 pages. Malacca, 1819.
11. 張遠兩友相論 Dialogues Between Chang and Yuen. 20 pages. Malacca, 1819.
12. 古今聖史記集 Sacred History. 71 pages. Malacca, 1819.
13. 受災學義論說 Duty of Men in Times of Public Calamity. 13 pages. Malacca, 1819.
14. 三寶仁會論 Three Benevolent Societies. 32 pages. Malacca, 1821.
15. 全地萬國紀略 Sketch of the World. 30 pages. Malacca, 1822.
16. 鄉訓五十二則 Twelve Village Sermons. 70 pages. Malacca, 1824.
17. 上帝聖教公會門 The Gate of God's Church. 30 pages, Malacca, [?].
18. 靈魂篇大全 Treatise on the Soul. 183 pages. Malacca, 1824.
19. 聖書節解 Commentary on Ephesians. 104 pages. Malacca, 1825.
20. 神天聖書 The Holy Bible. Malacca, 1824.
21. 察世俗每月統記傳 Chinese Monthly Magazine. 7 volumes. 524 leaves. Malacca, 1815–1821.

WORKS IN ENGLISH

22. *The Sacred Edict: Containing Sixteen Maxims of the Emperor Kang-he*. 299 pages. London, 1817.
23. *A Retrospect of the First Ten Years of the Protestant Mission to China, (Now, in Connection With the Malay, Denominated, the Ultra-Ganges Missions) Accompanied With Miscellaneous Remarks on the Literature, History, and Mythology of China, &c.* 384 pages. Malacca, 1820.

Appendix 4

24. *The Indo-Chinese Gleaner*. Quarterly magazine. Malacca, 1817–1822.

Appendix 5
Works of Liang Fa[1]

1. 救世錄撮要略解 Miscellaneous Exhortations. 37 pages. Canton, 1819.
2. 熟學聖理略論 Perfect Acquaintance With the Holy Doctrine [An Autobiography]. 9 pages. Canton, 1828.
3. 真道問答淺解 A Catechism on the Ten Commandments and the Duties of Christianity. 14 pages. Malacca, 1829.
4. 聖書日課初學便用 Scripture Lessons for the Young. 3 vols. Canton, 1831.
5. 勸世良言 Good Words Exhorting the Age. A collection of 9 tracts, revised by Robert Morrison, and printed at Canton in 1832. It has gained considerable celebrity, as being the work from which Hung Seu-tseuen is said to have gained his first knowledge of Christianity. The following is a summary of their contents:
    - (1) 真傳救世文 A True Account of the Salvation of Mankind.
    - (2) 崇真闢邪論 Following the True and Rejecting the False.

1. A catalogue of the works of Liang Fa was recorded under a different spelling "Leang Kung-Fa" in Wylie, *Memorials*, 21–25. This list of Liang's selected Chinese works are adopted from Wylie's catalogue.

Appendix 5

- (3) A Collection of Various Tracts: 真經聖理 The Holy Truths Contained in the True Scriptures, 代贖罪救世 On Redemption by Christ, 聖經神詩篇 Psalms from the Scriptures, 聖經以賽亞 Extract from Isaiah 45:521, 聖經創世篇 Extract from Genesis Chapter 1.
- (4) 聖經雜解 Miscellaneous Explanations of Holy Scripture.
- (5) 聖經雜論 Miscellaneous Statements Founded on the Holy Scriptures.
- (6) 熟學真理論 Perfect Acquaintance With the True Doctrine.
- (7) 安危獲福篇 On Obtaining Happiness Whether in Peace of Peril.
- (8) 真經格言 Excellent Sayings From the True Scriptures.
- (9) 古經輯要 Selections From the Ancient Scriptures.

These works were revised and reprinted at Malacca as nine separate tracts. Four of them were again reprinted with modifications at Singapore, in a collection, with the title 揀選勸世要言 Selection of Important Words to Admonish the Age, 62 pages. Another eclectic compilation, taken from most of the above tracts was published at Singapore, with the title 求福免禍要論 Important Discourse on Seeking Happiness and Escaping Misery. 82 pages.

6. 祈禱文讚神詩 Prayers and Hymns. 60 pages. Macao, 1833. This is the Morning service of the Church of England; the Prayers being composed by Liang Fa, pp. 44; and the Hymns by Morrison and others.

7. A sheet tract on the Vanity of Idols, taken from Isaiah chapter 44.

Bibliography

Anonymous. "Death of Dr. Milne." *American Baptist Magazine, and Missionary Intelligencer* 4.3 (1823) 109.
Anonymous. "Memoir of the Late Rev. George Cowie, of Huntly." *Evangelical Magazine* 19 (1811) 121–27.
Anonymous. "Memoir of William Milne." In *The Christian Library: A Reprint of Standard Religious Writings*, edited by Jonathan Going, et al., 3:413–16. New York: Thomas George, Jr., 1835.
Anonymous. "To Pious Young Men." *The Evangelical Magazine* (April 1805) 167–71.
Aprem, Mar. *Nestorian Theology*. Kerala, India: Mar Narsai, 1980.
Banner, James M., Jr. *Being a Historian: An Introduction to the Professional World of History*. New York: Cambridge University Press, 2012.
Barnett, Suzanne W. "Silent Evangelism: Presbyterians and the Missions Press in China, 1807–1860." *Journal of Presbyterian History* 49.4 (1971) 287–302.
Bays, Daniel H. *A New History of Christianity in China*. Malden, MA: Wiley-Blackwell, 2012.
———. "Christian Tracts: The Two Friends." In *Christianity in China: Early Protestant Missionary Writings*, edited by Suzanne Wilson Barnett and John King Fairbank, 19–34. Cambridge, MA: Harvard University Press, 1985.
———. "Milne, William." In *Biographical Dictionary of Christian Missions*, edited by Gerald H. Anderson, 461–62. Grand Rapids: Eerdmans, 1998.
Bebbington, David W. *Baptists Through the Centuries: A History of a Global People*. Waco, TX: Baylor University Press, 2010.
———. *Evangelicalism in Modern Britain: A History from the 1730s to the 1980s*. Reprint. London: Routledge, 2005.
———. *Patterns in History: A Christian Perspective on Historical Thought*. Grand Rapids: Baker, 1990.
Beck, Peter. *The Voice of Faith: Jonathan Edwards' Theology of Prayer*. Guelph, ON: Joshua, 2010.

Bibliography

Bennett, James. *Memoirs of the Life of the Rev[erend] David Bogue.* London: Frederick Westley and A. H. Davis, 1827.
Bernhardt, Kathryn. *Women and Property in China, 960-1949.* Stanford, CA: Stanford University Press, 1999.
Bezzant, Rhys. "'Singly, Particularly, Closely': Edwards as Mentor." *Jonathan Edwards Studies* 4.2 (2014) 228-46.
Bodde, Derk. "The State and Empire of Ch'in." In *The Cambridge History of China: The Ch'in and Han Empires 221 BC-AD 220*, edited by Denis Twitchett and Michael Loewe, 1:72-80. Cambridge: Cambridge University Press, 1986.
Bogue, David. *Objections Against a Mission to the Heathen, Stated and Considered; A Sermon, Preached at Tottenham Court Chapel, Before the Founders of the Missionary Society, 24 Sep[tember], 1795.* Cambridge: Hilliard and Metcalf, 1811.
Bohr, P. Richard. "The Heavenly Kingdom in China: Religion and the Taiping Revolution, 1837-1853." *Fides et Historia* 17.2 (1964) 38-52.
———. "The Legacy of William Milne." *IBMR* 25.4 (2001) 173-78.
———. "Liang Fa's *Quest for Moral Power*." In *Christianity In China: Early Protestant Missionary Writings*, edited by Suzanne Wilson Barnett and John King Fairbank, 35-46. Cambridge, MA: Harvard University Press, 1985.
Bonhoeffer, Dietrich. *The Cost of Discipleship.* New York: Touchstone, 1995.
Bonk, Jonathan James. "'All Things to All Men?' Protestant Missionary Identification in Theory and Practice, 1860-1910, with Special Reference to the London Missionary Society in Central Africa and Central China." PhD diss., University of Aberdeen, 1982.
Bosch, David J. *Transforming Mission: Paradigm Shifts in Theology of Mission.* American Society of Missiology Series 16. Reprint. Maryknoll, NY: Orbis, 2012.
Bridgman, Elijah Coleman. "A Brief Sketch of the Life and Labors of the Late Rev. William Milne, D.D." *CR* 1.8 (1832) 316-25.
———. "Review, The Sacred Edict." *CR* 1.8 (1832) 297-315.
Brown, Arthur Judson. *Rising Churches In Non-Christian Lands: Lectures Delivered on the College of Missions Lectureship, Indianapolis; The Severance Lectureship, Western Theological Seminary, Pittsburgh.* New York: Missionary Education Movement of the United States and Canada, 1915.
Brown, Stewart J. "Religion in Scotland." In *A Companion to Eighteenth-Century Britain*, edited by H. T. Dickinson, 260-70. Malden, MA: Blackwell, 2002.
Burleigh, J. H. S. *A Church History of Scotland.* London: Oxford University Press, 1860.
Campbell, John. "The Rev. John Hill, M.A., of Huntly." *The Christian Witness and Church Member's Magazine* 6 (1849) 16-18.
Campbell, R. H. "Cowie, George." In *Dictionary of Evangelical Biography 1730-1860*, edited by Donald M. Lewis, 261. Peabody, MA: Hendrickson, 2004.

Bibliography

Carey, Hilary M. *God's Empire: Religion and Colonialism in the British World, c. 1801-1908.* Cambridge: Cambridge University Press, 2011.

Carey Study Centre. "The Charter Act of 1813." Carey Study Centre, http://www.wmcarey.edu/carey/wmward/Main%20html/seram19.html (accessed on October 29, 2013).

Carwardine, Richard. *Transatlantic Revivalism: Popular Evangelicalism in Britain and America, 1790-1865.* Milton Keynes, England: Paternoster, 1978.

Chang, Chu-ling. "Chung-Hua Ti-I-Tz'u Shou-His-Jen Ts'ai Kao Hsien-Sheng I-Shih 中國第一次受洗人蔡高先生軼事 [Anecdotes of Mr. Ts'ai Kao, the First Baptized Chinese]." In *China Church Year Book 1915*, 154-56. Shanghai: Commercial, 1915.

Chao, Jonathan. "Church and State in China, 1949-1988." In *Wise as Serpents and Gentle as Doves*, edited by Richard van Houten, vii-xxxiv. Hong Kong: Chinese Church Research Center, 1988.

———. *A History of the Church in Church Since 1949; A Reader: An Expanded Study Guide.* Grand Rapids: Institute of Theological Studies, 1995.

Charbonnier, Jean-Pierre. *Christians in China: A.D. 600 to 2000.* Translated by M. N. L. Couve de Murville. San Francisco: Ignatius, 2007.

Chu, Yiu Kwong. "Between Unity and Diversity: The Role of William Milne in the Development of the Ultra-Ganges Missions." MPhil diss., Hong Kong Baptist University, 1999.

Church Missionary Society. *The Missionary Register for the Year 1814: Containing an Abstract of the Proceeding of the Principal Missionary and Bible Societies Throughout the World.* Vol. 2. London: Ellerton and Henderson, 1814.

Clark, Ian D. L. "From Protest to Reaction: The Moderate Regime in the Church of Scotland, 1752-1805." In *Essays in Scottish History in the Eighteenth Century*, edited by N. T. Phillipson and Rosalind Mitchison, 200-24. Edinburgh: Edinburgh University Press, 1970.

Clark, William H. *The Church in China: Its Vitality, Its Future?* New York: Council Press of the National Council of the Churches of Christ in the USA, 1970.

Cohen, Paul A. "Missionary Approaches: Hudson Taylor and Timothy Richard." *Papers on China* 11 (1957) 29-62.

Conforti, Joseph. "Joseph Bellamy and the New Divinity Movement." *New England Historical and Genealogical Register* 137 (1983) 126-38.

———. "The Rise of the New Divinity in Western New England, 1740-1800." *Historical Journal of Western Massachusetts* 8 (1980) 37-47.

Conn, Harvie M. "Contextual Theologies: The Problem of Agendas." *Westminster Theological Journal* 52 (1990) 51-63.

Cook, Richard R., and David W. Pao, eds. *After Imperialism: Christian Identity in China and the Global Evangelical Movement.* Eugene, OR: Pickwick, 2011.

Corrie, Daniel. *A Sermon Preached at the Parish Church of St. Andrew by the Wardrobe and St. Anne Blackfriars, on Tuesday, April 30, 1816, Before the*

Bibliography

Church Missionary Society For Africa and the East, Being Their Sixteenth Anniversary. London: Whittingham and Rowland, 1816.

Cowie, George. *The Dissenter's Guide in Choosing a Pastor: Pointing Necessary Qualifications of a Gospel Minister, and How to be Able to Distinguish Those that are Possessed of Them; In a Letter to the Seceders.* Rev. ed. Edinburgh: Maccliesh, 1799.

Cowper, William. "Light Shining Our of the Darkness." In *Twenty-Six Letters on Religious Subjects*, Omicron [John Newton], 3rd ed., 295. London: W. Oliver, 1887.

Cross, F. L., and E. A. Lingston, eds. "Antiburgher." In *Oxford Dictionary of the Christian Church*, 7. Rev. ed. Oxford: Oxford University Press, 2005.

Daily, Christopher Allen. "From Gosport to Canton: A New Approach to Robert Morrison and the Beginnings of Protestant Missions in China." PhD diss., University of London, 2010.

———. *Robert Morrison and the Protestant for China.* Hong Kong: Hong Kong University Press, 2013.

Darwin, John. *Unfinished Empire: The Global Expansion of Britain.* London: Allen Lane, 2012.

De Witt, Dennis. *History of the Dutch in Malaysia.* Reprint. Malaysia: Nutmeg, 2011.

Di Gangi, Mariano. *Meaning of Christian Discipleship.* Agincourt, ON: Bible & Medical Missionary Fellowship, 1975.

Diary of Liang Fa, Special Archive and Collection, CWM South China Journal Box 1, 14A Liang Afa, South China 1830 March 28–Nov 6, Chinese Original of no. 14, SOAS Library, London.

Doran, Christine. "'A Fine Sphere for Female Usefulness': Missionary Women in the Straits Settlements, 1815–45." *Journal of the Malaysian Branch of the Royal Asiatic Society* 69.1 (1996) 100–11.

Doyle, G. Wright. "Names for 'God': Shangdi." *Global China Center.* Web. http://www.globalchinacenter.org/analysis/articles/names-for-god-shang-di.php (accessed on December 12, 2014).

———. "Names for 'God': Shen." *Global China Center.* Web. http://www.globalchinacenter.org/analysis/articles/names-for-god-shen.php (accessed on December 12, 2014).

Duesing, Jason G., ed. *Adoniram Judson: A Bicentennial Appreciation of the Pioneer American Missionary.* Nashville: B & H, 2012.

Eccles, L., and Sam Lieu, trans. "Da Qin Jing Jiao Liu Xing Zhong Guo Bei [The Nestorian Stele]: Stele on the Diffusion of the Luminous Religion of Dao Qin (Rome) in the Middle Kingdom." Macquarie University, http://mq.edu.au/pubstatic/public/download.jsp?id=72496 (accessed on October 29, 2013).

Editorial. "The East India Company: The Company That Ruled the Waves, as State-Backed Firms Once Again Become Forces in Global Business, We Ask What They Can Learn From the Greatest of Them All." *Economist*,

Bibliography

http://www.economist.com/node/21541753 (accessed on October 29, 2013).

Ellis, William. *The History of the London Missionary Society*. Vol. 1. London: John Snow, 1844.

Fairbank, John K. "China's World Order: The Tradition of Chinese Foreign Relations." *Encounter* 27.6 (1966) 14–20.

Fairbank, John K., ed. *Late Ch'ing 1800–1911, Part 1*. The Cambridge History of China 10. Cambridge: Cambridge University Press, 1978.

Fairbank, John K., and Kwang-Ching Liu, eds. *Late Ch'ing, 1800–1911, Part 2*. The Cambridge History of China 11. Cambridge: Cambridge University Press, 1980.

Farrer, Keith. *William Carey: Missionary and Botanist*. Victoria, Australia: Carey Baptist Grammar School, 2005.

Fawcett, Arthur. *The Cambuslang Revival: The Scottish Evangelical Revival of the Eighteenth Century*. Edinburgh: Banner of Truth, 1971.

Fea, John. *Why Study History? Reflecting on the Importance of the Past*. Grand Rapids: Baker, 2013.

Fisher, Edward, and Thomas Boston. *The Marrow of Modern Divinity: The Sixteenth Edition, With Notes*. Glasgow: John Bryce, 1766.

Foley, Toshikazu S. *Biblical Translation in Chinese and Greek: Verbal Aspect in Theory and Practice*. Leiden, Netherlands: Brill, 2009.

Foster, John. "The Christian Origins of the Taiping Rebellion." *International Review of Mission* 40.158 (1951) 156–67.

Frey, Joseph Samuel C. F., ed. *Theological Lectures of the Late Rev[erend] David Bogue, D. D. Never Before Published*. New York: Lewis Colby, 1849.

George, Timothy. "Evangelical Revival and the Missionary Awakening." In *The Great Commission: Evangelicals and the History of World Missions*, edited by Martin I. Klauber and Scott M. Manetsch, 44–63. Nashville: B & H, 2008.

Gibbard, Noel. "David Bogue and the Gosport Academy." *Foundations* 20 (1988) 36–41.

Grudem, Wayne. *Systematic Theology: An Introduction to Biblical Doctrine*. Grand Rapids: Zondervan, 1994.

Haines, J. Harry. "A History of Protestant Missions in Malaya During the Nineteenth Century, 1815–1881." ThD diss., Princeton Theological Seminary, 1962.

Haldane, Alexander. *Memoirs of the Lives of Robert Haldane of Airthrey, and of His Brother, James Alexander Haldane*. Edinburgh: W. Whyte, 1852.

Han, L. N. "The Historical Status of Sup Sam Hung in the Cultural Exchange Between China and the West." *Journal of Guangzhou University* 5.8 (2006) 61–64.

Hanan, Patrick. *Chinese Fiction of the Nineteenth and Early Twentieth Centuries*. New York: Columbia University Press, 2004.

Hancock, Christopher. *Robert Morrison and the Birth of Chinese Protestantism*. New York: T & T Clark, 2008.

Bibliography

Harcus, A. Drummond. "History of the Presbyterian Church in Malaya." *The Journal of the Presbyterian Historical Society of England* 10.4 (1955) 160–75.

Harrison, Brian. *Waiting For China: The Anglo-Chinese College at Malacca, 1818–1843, and Early Nineteenth-Century Missions*. Hong Kong: Hong Kong University Press, 1979.

Haykin, Michael A. G. "'A Dull Flint': Andrew Fuller--Rope-Holder, Critic of Hyper-Calvinism & Missionary Pioneer." *Andrew Fuller Center for Baptist Studies*. Web. http://www.andrewfullercenter.org/files/Andrew-fuller.pdf (accessed on November 1, 2013).

———. *"At the Pure Foundation of Thy Word": Andrew Fuller as an Apologist*. Eugene, OR: Wipf & Stock, 2006.

———. "Just Before Judson: The Significance of William Carey's Life, Thought, and Ministry." In *Adoniram Judson: A Bicentennial Appreciation of the Pioneer American Missionary*, edited by Jason G. Duesing, 9–30. Nashville: B & H, 2012.

———, and Kenneth J. Stewart, eds. *The Emergence of Evangelicalism: Exploring Historical Continuities*. Nashville: B & H, 2008.

Henry, Carl F. H. *God, Revelation and Authority*. Waco, TX: Word Books, 1976.

———. *Toward a Recovery of Christian Belief: The Rutherford Lectures*. Wheaton, IL: Crossway, 1990.

Hensley, J. "Bellamy, Joseph." In *Biographical Dictionary of Evangelicals*, edited by Timothy Larsen and Mark A. Noll. Downers Grove, IL: InterVarsity, 2003.

Hesselgrave, David J. *Planting Churches Cross-Culturally: North America and Beyond*. Grand Rapids: Baker, 2000.

Hill, Jonathan, ed. *Zondervan Handbook to the History of Christianity*. Grand Rapids: Zondervan, 2006.

Hindmarsh, D. Bruce. *The Evangelical Conversion Narrative: Spiritual Autobiography in Early Modern England*. Oxford: Oxford University Press, 2005.

Hoehl, Stacy E. "The Mentor Relationships: An Exploration of Paul as Loving Mentor to Timothy and the Application of This Relationship to Contemporary Leadership Challenges." *Journals of Biblical Perspectives in Leadership* 3.2 (2011) 32–47.

Hsu, Immanuel C. Y. *The Rise of Modern China*. Oxford: Oxford University Press, 2000.

Hu, Kesen. "Comparative Studies on 'Contention of a Hundred Schools of Thought' and 'the May Fourth' New Culture Movement." *Journal of Shaoyang University* 11.1 (2012) 83–95.

Hucker, Charles O. *China's Imperial Past: An Introduction to Chinese History and Culture*. Stanford, CA: Stanford University Press, 1975.

Hussin, Nordin. *Trade and Society in the Straits of Melaka: Dutch Meleka and English Penang, 1780–1830*. Copenhagen, Denmark: Nordic Institute of

Bibliography

Asian Studies Press; Singapore: National University of Singapore Press, 2007.

Johnston, John C. *Treasury of the Scottish Covenant.* Edinburgh: Andrew Elliot, 1887.

Journal of William Milne, 1815–1817, Special Archive and Collection, CWM South China Journals Box 1, 13 W Milne, South Chin (1815–1817, Dec 30–Jan 4), Malacca, SOAS Library, London.

Kidd, Thomas S. *The Great Awakening: The Roots of Evangelical Christianity in Colonial America.* New Haven, CT: Yale University Press, 2007.

Kitzan, Laurence. "The London Missionary Society in India and China, 1798–1834." PhD diss., University of Toronto, 1965.

Kim, Sukjoo. "Liang Fa's Quanshi Liangyan and Its Impact On the Taiping Movement." PhD diss., Baylor University, 2011.

Kinniburgh, Robert, ed. *Fathers of Independency in Scotland; Or, Biographical Sketches of Early Scottish Congregational Ministers. A.D. 1798–1851.* Edinburgh; Glasgow; London: A. Fullarton, 1851.

Klauber, Martin I., and Scott M. Manetsch, eds. *The Great Commission: Evangelicals and the History of World Missions.* Nashville: B & H, 2008.

Kling, David W., and Douglas A. Sweeney, eds. *Jonathan Edwards at Home and Abroad: Historical Memories, Cultural Movements, Global Horizons.* Columbia, SC: University of South Carolina Press, 2003.

Kong, Bobby Sng Ewe. "Leong Kung Fa." In *A Dictionary of Asian Christianity*, edited by Scott W. Sunquist, 482. Grand Rapids: Eerdmans, 2001.

Kuhn, Philip A. *Rebellion and Its Enemies in Late Imperial China; Militarization and Social Structure, 1796–1864.* Cambridge, MA: Harvard University Press, 1970.

Kwok, Benedict H. "Moltmann's Method of Theological Construction." In *Sino-Theology and the Thinking of Jürgen Moltmann Sino-Theologie und das Denken Jürgen Moltmanns*, edited by Jürgen Moltmann and Thomas Tseng, 1–24. Frankfurt am Main: Peter Lang, 2004.

Lachman, David C. *The Marrow Controversy 1718–1723: A Historical and Theological Analysis.* Edinburgh: Rutherford House, 1988.

Lai, John Tsz-Pang. "Christian Literature in Nineteenth-Century China Missions—A Priority? Or An Optional Extra?" *International Bulletin of Missionary Research* 32.2 (2008) 71–76.

———. "The Enterprise of Translating Christian Tracts by Protestant Missionaries in Nineteenth-Century China." PhD diss., University of Oxford, 2005.

Lai, Pan-Chiu. "Sino-Theology as a Non-Church Movement: Historical and Comparative Perspective." In *Christian Presence and Progress in North-East China: Historical and Comparative Studies*, edited by Jan A. B. Jongeneel et al., 87–103. Frankfurt am Main: Peter Lang, 2011.

———. "Sino-Theology, the Bible, and the Christian Tradition." *Studies in World Christianity* 12 (2006) 266–81.

Bibliography

Lai, Pan-Chiu, and Jason T. S. Lam. "Retrospect and Prospect of Sino-Christian Theology: An Introduction." In *Sino-Christian Theology*, edited Pan-Chiu Lai and Jason Lam, 1–17. Frankfurt am Main: Peter Lang, 2010.

Lai, Whalen W. "The First Chinese Christian Gospel: Liang A-Fa's 'Good Words to Admonish the World.'" *Ching Feng* 38.2 (1995) 83–105.

Latourette, Kenneth Scott. *A History of Christian Missions in China*. New York: Macmillan, 1929.

———. *The Great Century in Northern Africa and Asia A.D. 1800–A.D. 1914*. A History of the Expansion of Christianity 6. New York: Harper, 1944.

Lau, Hua Teck. "The Cross and the Lotus." *Church & Society* 6.2 (2003) 85–99.

Law, Alexander. "Scottish Schoolbooks of the Eighteenth and Nineteenth Centuries." *Studies in Scottish Literature* 18.1 (1983) 1–32.

Lawless, Chuck. "Paul and Leadership Development." In *Paul's Missionary Methods: In His Time and Ours*, edited by Robert L. Plummer and John Mark Terry, 216–34. Downers Grove, IL: InterVarsity, 2012.

Lee, Archie C. C. "God's Asian Names: Rendering the Biblical God in Chinese." SBL Forum, http://sbl-site.org/Article.aspx?ArticleID=456 (accessed on November 23, 2014).

Li, Zhigang. *History of Early Christian Missionary in China* (基督教早期在華宣教史). Taiwan: Commercial Press, 1985.

Limberis, Vasiliki. *Divine Heiress: The Virgin Mary and the Creation of Christian Constantinople*. London; New York: Routledge, 1994.

London Missionary Society. "Malacca." *Missionary Sketches* 54 (July 1831) 2–4.

———. "Sketch of the Chinese Mission." *Missionary Sketches* 9 (April 1820) 2–4.

———. "Sketch of the Malacca Mission and Anglo-Chinese College." *Missionary Sketches* 28 (January 1825) 2–4.

———. "Sketch of the Society's Mission at Pulo Pinang, or Prince of Wales' Island." *Missionary Sketches* 37 (April 1827) 2–4.

Longenecker, Richard N., ed. *Patterns of Discipleship in the New Testament*. Grand Rapids: Eerdmans, 1996.

Lovelace, Richard F. *Dynamics of Spiritual Life: An Evangelical Theology of Renewal*. Downers Grove, IL: InterVarsity, 1979.

Lovett, Richard. *History of the London Missionary Society 1795–1895*. London: Henry Frowde, 1899.

Löwith, Karl. *Meaning in History*. Chicago, IL: University of Chicago Press, 1949.

Lucas, Sean Michael. "'A Man Just Like Us': Jonathan Edwards and Spiritual Formation for Ministerial Candidates." *Eusebeia* 2 (2004) 29–41.

MacInnis, Donald E. "Liang Fa." In *Biographical Dictionary of Christian Missions*, edited Gerald H. Anderson. Grand Rapids: Eerdmans, 1998.

Mackelvie, William. *Annals and Statistics of the United Presbyterian Church*. Edinburgh: Oliphant and Andrew Elliot, 1873.

Makidon, Michael D. "The Marrow Controversy." *Journal of the Grace Evangelical Society* 16.31 (2003) 65–77.

Bibliography

Mao, Zedong. *Collected Writings of Chairman Mao: Politics and Tactics.* Edited Shawn Conners. El Pasco, TX: El Pasco Norte, 2009.

Markus, Robert A. "History." In *Augustine Through the Ages: An Encyclopedia,* edited by Allan D. Fitzgerald, 433. Grand Rapids: Eerdmans, 1999.

McClymond, Michael J., and Gerald R. McDermott. *The Theology of Jonathan Edwards.* New York: Oxford University Press, 2012.

McGowan, A. T. B. "Evangelism in Scotland From Knox to Cunningham." In *The Emergence of Evangelicalism: Exploring Historical Continuities,* edited by Michael A. G. Haykin and Kenneth J. Stewart, 63–83. Nottingham, England: Apollos, 2008.

McGowan, A. T. B. *The Federal Theology of Thomas Boston.* Carlisle, UK: Paternoster; Edinburgh: Rutherford House, 1997.

McGrath, Alister E., ed. *The Christian Theology Reader.* 2nd ed. Malden, MA: Blackwell, 2001.

McIntosh, John R. *Church and Theology in Enlightenment Scotland: The Popular Party, 1740–1800.* East Linton, Scotland: Tuckwell, 1998.

McNeur, George Hunter. *China's First Preacher Liang A-Fa 1789–1855.* Shanghai: Kwang Hsueh, 1934.

Michael, Franz, and Chung-li Chang, coll. *The Taiping Rebellion: History and Documents.* Translated by Margery Anneberg; edited by Gladys Greenwood. Seattle: University of Washington, 1972.

Milne, William. *A Catechism for Youth* 幼學淺解問答. Malacca: Anglo-Chinese, 1817.

———. "Account of a Secret Association in China, Entitled the Triad Society." *Transactions of the Royal Asiatic Society of Great Britain and Ireland* 1.2 (1826) 240–50.

———. "Annals of Canton." *Indo-Chinese Gleaner* 22 (1822) 280–85.

———. *A Retrospect of the First Ten Years of the Protestant Mission to China.* Malacca: Anglo-Chinese Press, 1820.

———. *Dialogues Between Chang and Yuen* 張遠兩友相論. Hong Kong: Anglo-Chinese College, 1851.

———. "Memoir of Mrs. Milne." *Indo-Chinese Gleaner* 8 (April 1819) 103–15.

———, and George Thom. *The Ordination Services of the Rev. William Milne and the Rev. George Thom; Missionaries to the East 1812.* Aberdeen: D. Chalmers, 1813.

Milne, William C[harles]. *Life in China.* London: G. Routledge, 1857.

Minkema, Kenneth P. "'Informing of the Child's Understanding, Influencing His Heart, and Directing Its Practice': Jonathan Edwards on Education." *Acta Theologica* 31.2 (2011) 159–89.

———. "Jonathan Edwards on Education and His Educational Legacy." In *After Jonathan Edwards: The Courses of the New England Theology,* edited by Oliver C. Crisp and Douglas A. Sweeney. New York: Oxford University Press, 2012.

Bibliography

Mitchell, Christopher Wayne. "Jonathan Edwards's Scottish Connection and the Eighteenth-Century Scottish Evangelical Revival, 1735–1750." PhD diss., University of St. Andrews, 1997.

———. "Jonathan Edwards's Scottish Connection." In *Jonathan Edwards at Home and Abroad: Historical Memories, Cultural Movements, Global Horizons*, edited by David W. Kling and Douglas A. Sweeney, 222–47. Columbia, SC: University of South Carolina Press, 2003.

M'Millan, Samuel, ed. *Complete Works of the Late Rev[erend] Thomas Boston, Ettrick*. Reprint. Wheaton, IL: Richard Owen Roberts, 1980.

Mordon, Peter. "Andrew Fuller as an Apologist for Missions." In *'At the Pure Foundation of Thy Word': Andrew Fuller as an Apologist*, edited by Michael A. G. Haykin, 237–55. Eugene, OR: Wipf & Stock, 2004.

Morrison, Eliza A. *Memoirs of the Life and Labours of Robert Morrison*. London: Longman, Orme, Brown, Green, and Longmans, 1839.

Morrison, Robert. *A Parting Memorial; Consisting of Miscellaneous Discourses, Written and Preached in China; At Singapore; On Board Ship at Sea, in the Indian Ocean; At the Cape of Good Hope; and in England*. London: W. Simpkin and R. Marshall, 1826.

———. *Memoirs of the Rev. William Milne, D.D. Late Missionary to China and Principal of the Anglo-Chinese College; Compiled From Documents Written by the Deceased; To Which are Added Occasional Remarks*. Malacca: The Mission, 1824.

———. *To the Public, Concerning the Anglo-Chinese College*. Malacca: The Mission, 1823.

Mulholland, Kenneth B. "From Luther to Carey: Pietism and the Modern Missionary Movement." *Bibliotheca Sacra* 156.621 (1999) 85–95.

Mungello, D. E., ed. *The Chinese Rites Controversy: Its History and Meaning*. Monumenta Serica Monograph Series 33. Nettetal, Germany: Steyler Verlag, 1994.

Neill, Stephen. *A History of Christian Missions*. 2nd ed. New York: Penguin, 1986.

Nettles, Thomas. *By His Grace and For His Glory: A Historical, Theological, and Practical Study of the Doctrines of Grace in Baptist Life*. Rev. ed. Cape Coral, FL: Founders, 2006.

Newton, John. *Twenty-Six Letters on Religious Subjects*. 3rd ed. London: W. Oliver, 1887.

Norris, Richard A., Jr., trans. *The Christological Controversy*. Philadelphia: Fortress, 1980.

Oak, Sung-Deuk. "Competing Chinese Names for God: The Chinese Term Question and Its Influence Upon Korea." *Journal of Korean Religions* 3.2 (2012) 89–115.

———. *The Making of Korean Christianity: Protestant Encounters With Korean Religions, 1876–1915*. Waco, TX: Baylor University Press, 2013.

Oh, Soon-Bang. "The Spread and Translation of Chinese Christian Novels in the 1890s' Korea," *Dong Hwa Journal of Humanities* 9 (2006) 215–50.

Bibliography

Old, Hughes Oliphant. *The Modern Age*. Vol. 6 of *The Reading and Preaching of the Scriptures in the Worship of the Christian Church*. Grand Rapids: Eerdmans, 2007.

O'Sullivan, Leona. "The London Missionary Society: A Written Record of Missionaries and Printing Presses in the Straits Settlements, 1815–1847." *Journal of the Malaysian Branch of the Royal Asiatic Society* 57.2 (1984) 61–104.

Oussoren, Aalbertinus Hermen. *William Carey, Especially His Missionary Principles*. Leiden, Netherlands: A. W. Sijthoff's Uitgeversmaatschapppij, 1945.

Packer, J. I. *Evangelism and the Sovereignty of God*. Downers Grove, IL: InterVarsity, 2008.

Pan, Jianqi 潘建齊. "On the Influence of Good Words for Exhorting the Age on Hong Xiuquan." MA diss., National Cheng Kung University, 2007.

Paquette, Jean. "An Uncompromising Land: the London Missionary Society in China, 1807–1860." PhD diss., University of California, 1987.

Pastoor, Charles, and Galen K. Johnson. *The A to Z of the Puritans*. Lanham, MD: Scarecrow, 2009.

Perrier, Pierre, and Xavier Walter. *Thomas Fonde L'Eglise en Chine (65–68 Ap. J-C)*. Paris, France: Editions du Jubilé, 2008.

Peyrefitte, Alain. *The Immobile Empire*. New York: Vintage, 2013.

Philip, Robert. *Baptism For the Dead, In China; Or A Voice From the Tombs of Morrison And Milne, To the Schools of the Prophets*. London: Thomas Ward, 1835.

———. *The Life and Opinion of the Rev. William Milne, D.D, Missionary to China, Illustrated By Biographical Annals of Asiatic Missions, From Primitive to Protestant Times; Intended As A Guide to Missionary Spirit*. London: John Snow, 1840.

———. *The Life and Times of the Reverend George Whitefield*. London: George Virtue; Bungay: J. R. and C. Childs, 1838.

Piggin, Stuart. *Making Evangelical Missionaries 1789–1858: The Social Background, Motives and Training of British Protestant Missionaries to India*. Abingdon, UK: Sutton Courtenay, 1984.

Platt, Stephen R. *Autumn In The Heavenly Kingdom: China, the West, and the Epic Story of the Taiping Civil War*. New York: Vintage, 2012.

Plummer, Robert L., and John Mark Terry, eds. *Paul's Missionary Methods: In His Time and Ours*. Downers Grove, IL: InterVaristy, 2012.

Reed, Andrew, and Charles Reed, eds. *Memoris of the Life and Philanthropic Labours of Andrew Reed, D.D., With Selections from His Journals*. London: Strahan, 1863.

Riegert, Ray, and Thomas Moore, eds. *The Lost Sutras of Jesus: Unlocking the Ancient Wisdom of the Xian Monks*. Translated by John Babcock. Berkeley, CA: Seastone, 2003.

Bibliography

Ricci, Matteo. *On Friendship: One Hundred Maxims for a Chinese Prince.* Translated by Timothy Billings. New York: Columbia University Press, 2009.

Robert Morrison to G. Burder, Canton, January 1, 1816, Special Archive and Collection, CWM/LMS/CH/SC/01/04/C, SOAS Library, London.

Roxborogh, John. "Milne, William." In *A Dictionary of Asian Christianity,* edited by Scott W. Sunquist, 551. Grand Rapids: Eerdmans, 2001.

Rowold, Henry. "Robert Morrison Pioneer China Missionary Observing the Bicentennial." *Misso Apstolica* 15.2 (2007) 103–11.

Royal Commissioners. *Second Report of the Commissioners Appoinyed by His Majesty William IV, November 23rd, 1836; and Re-appointed by Her Majesty Victoria I, October 2nd, 1837; For Visiting the Universities of King's College and Marischal College, Aberdeen.* London: W. Clowes, 1839.

Rubinstein, Murray A. *The Origins of the Anglo-American Missionary Enterprise in China, 1807–1840.* ATLA Monograph Series 33. Lanham, MD: Scarecrow, 1996.

Rule, Paul A. "The Chinese Rites Controversy: A Long Lasting Controversy in Sino-Western Cultural History." *Pacific Rim Report* 32 (2004) 2–8.

Ruokanen, Miikka, and Paulos Huang, ed. *Christianity and Chinese Culture.* Grand Rapids: Eerdmans, 2010.

Saeki, P. Y. *The Nestorian Documents and Relics in China.* Tokyo, Japan: Academy of Oriental Culture Tokyo Institute, 1951.

Schaff, Philip, ed. *The Creeds of Christendom With a History and Critical Notes.* Grand Rapids: Baker, 1983.

Schmidt, Leigh Eric. *Holy Fairs: Scotland and the Making of American Revivalism.* Rev. ed. Grand Rapids: Eerdmans, 2001.

Seton, Rosemary E. *Western Daughters in Eastern Lands: British Missionary Women in Asia.* Santa Barbara, CA: Praeger, 2013.

Shaw, Ian J. "The Evangelical Revival Through the Eyes of the 'Evangelical Century': Nineteenth Century Perceptions of the Origins of Evangelicalism." In *The Emergence of Evangelicalism: Exploring Historical Continuities,* edited by Michael A. G. Haykin and Kenneth J. Stewart, 302–323. Nottingham, England: Apollos, 2008.

Sivasundaram, Sujit. *Nature and the Godly Empire: Science and Evangelical Mission in the Pacific, 1795–1850.* Cambridge, England: Cambridge University Press, 2005.

Smith, A. Christopher. "A Tale of Many Models: The Missiological Significance of the Serampore Trio." *Missiology* 20.4 (1992) 479–500.

———. "The Edinburgh Connection: Between the Serampore Mission and Western Missiology." *Missiology* 18.2 (1990) 185–209.

Smither, Edward L. *Augustine as Mentor: A Model for Preparing Spiritual Leaders.* Nashville: B & H, 2008.

Song, Lihua. *Chinese Missionary Novel Studies* 傳教士漢文小說研究. Shanghai: Ancient Books, 2010.

Bibliography

———. "The Modern Development of Chinese Missionary Novels and Chinese Literature (傳教士漢文小說與中國文學的現代變革)." *Literary Criticism* 文學評論 1 (2011) 57–62.

———. "The Spread and Influence of the First Chinese Missionary Novel: Studies on William Milne's *Dialogues Between Chang and Yuen* (第一部傳教士中文小說的流傳與影響--米憐《張遠兩友相論》論略)." *Institute of Literature, Chinese Academy of Social Sciences*. Web. http://www.literature.org.cn/Article.aspx?id=8730 (accessed on February 13, 2014).

Spence, Jonathan D. *God's Chinese Son: The Taiping Heavenly Kingdom of Hong Xiuquan*. New York: W. W. Norton, 1996.

———. *The Memory Palace of Matteo Ricci*. New York: Penguin, 1985.

Stanley, Brian. "Horne, Melville." In *Biographical Dictionary of Christian Missions*, ed. Gerald H. Anderson, 304. New York: Macmillan, 1998.

Starke, Ekkehard. "Discipleship: 2. Systematic Theology." In *Encyclopedia of Christianity*, edited by Geoffrey W. Bromiley, 1:851–53. Grand Rapids: Eerdmans, 1999.

Starr, Chloë, ed. *Reading Christian Scriptures In China*. New York: T & T Clark, 2008.

Stevens, Edwin. "A Brief Sketch of the Life and Labors of the Late Rev. William Milne, D.D." *Chinese Repository* 1 (1832) 316–25.

Su, Ching. *Open Up, China! Studies on Robert Morrison and His Circle* 中國，開門！馬禮遜及相關人物研究. Ching Feng Series 14. Hong Kong: Christian Study Centre on Chinese Religion and Culture, 2005.

———. "The First Protestant Convert of China, Tsae A-ko (1788–1818)." *Ching Feng* 5.2 (2004) 227–43.

———. "The Printing Press of The London Missionary Society Among the Chinese." PhD diss., University of London, 1996.

Sumiko, Yamamoto. *History of Protestantism in China: The Indigenization of Christianity*. Tokyo, Japan: Toho Gakkai (Istitute of Eastern Culture), 2000.

Sunshine, Glenn. "William Carey (1761–1834)." *Chuck Colson Center for Christian Worldview*. Web. http://www.colsoncenter.org/the-center/columns/indepth/17309-william-carey-1761-1834 (accessed on October 29, 2013).

Sweeney, Douglas A., and Brandon G. Withrow. "Jonathan Edwards: Continuator or Pioneer of Evangelical History?" In *The Advent of Evangelicalism: Exploring Historical Continuities*, edited by Michael A. G. Haykin and Kenneth J. Stewart, 278–301. Nashville: B & H, 2008.

Terpstra, Chester. "David Bogue, D. D., 1750–1825: Pioneer and Missionary Educator." PhD diss., University of Edinburgh, 1959.

Terry, John Mark. "Paul and Indigenous Missions." In *Paul's Missionary Methods: In His Time and Ours*, edited by Robert L. Plummer and John Mark Terry, 160–74. Downers Grove, IL: InterVarsity, 2012.

Bibliography

Thompson, David M. "The Great Ejection of 1662: Memories, Interpretations and Justifications Within Protestant Dissent, 1662–2012." *Ecclesiology* 9.2 (2013) 161–82.

Tiedemann, R. G. "China and Its Neighbours." In *A World History of Christianity*, ed. Adrian Hastings. Grand Rapids: Eerdmans, 1999.

Tomlin, J. *Missionary Journals and Letters, Written During Eleven Years' Residence and Travels Amongst the Chinese, Siamese, Javanese, Khassias, and Other Eastern Nations*. London: James Nisbet, 1844.

Torrance, Thomas F. *Scottish Theology: From John Knox to John McLeod Campbell*. Edinburgh: T & T Clark, 1996.

Townsend, William John. *Robert Morrison: The Pioneer of Chinese Missions*. London: S.W. Partridge, 1890.

Turnbull, Ralph G. *Jonathan Edwards the Preacher*. Grand Rapids: Baker, 1958.

Van Den Berg, Johannes. *Constrained by Jesus' Love: An Inquiry into the Motives of the Missionary Awakening in Great Britain in the Period Between 1698 and 1815*. Kampen, Overijssel: J. H. Kok, 1956.

VanDoodewaard, William. *The Marrow Controversy and Seceder Tradition: Marrow Theology in the Associate Presbytery and Associate Synod Secession Churches of Scotland (1733–1799)*. Grand Rapids: Reformation Heritage, 2011.

Van Houten, Richard, ed. *Wise as Serpents and Gentle as Doves*. Pasadena, CA: W. Carey Library; Hong Kong: Chinese Church Research Center, 1988.

Vedder, Henry C. *A Short History of Baptist Missions*. Philadelphia: Judson, 1927.

W. B. R. W. "Notable Men & Women of Banffshire." *Scottish Notes and Queries* 6.8 (January 1893) 122.

Wagner, Rudolf G. *Reenacting the Heavenly Vision: The Role of Religion in the Taiping Rebellion*. Berkley, CA: University of California, Institute of East Asian Studies, 1982.

Walker, James. *The Theology and Theologians of Scotland Chiefly of the Seventeenth Century and Eighteenth Centuries*. Edinburgh: T & T Clark, 1888.

Walls, Andrew F. "Missions and Historical Memory: Jonathan Edwards and David Brainerd." In *Jonathan Edwards at Home and Abroad: Historical Memories, Cultural Movements, Global Horizons*, edited by David W. Kling and Douglas A. Sweeney, 248–65. Columbia, SC: University of South Carolina Press, 2003.

———. *The Missionary Movement in Christian History: Studies in the Transmission of Faith*. Maryknoll, NY: Orbis Books, 1996.

Westad, Odd Arne. *Restless Empire: China and the World Since 1750*. New York: Basic, 2012.

Westminster Assembly of Divines. "The Westminster Confession of Faith, 1647." In *The Creeds of Christendom With a History and Critical Notes*, edited by Philip Schaff. Grand Rapids: Baker, 1983.

Bibliography

Wheeler, E. M. "Were the Taipings 'Chinese Hussites'?." *Communio Vitaorum* 7.2 (1964) 223–24.
Whitney, Don. "Pursuing a Passion for God Through Spiritual Disciplines: Learning from Jonathan Edwards." In *A God Entranced Vision of All Things: The Legacy of Jonathan Edwards*, edited by John Piper and Justin Taylor. Wheaton, IL: Crossway, 2004.
Wilkins, Michael J. "Disciple, Discipleship." In *Evangelical Dictionary of World Missions*, edited by A. Scott Moreau, 279. Grand Rapids: Baker, 2000.
———. *Discipleship in the Ancient World and Matthew's Gospel*. Rev. ed. Grand Rapids: Baker, 1995.
William Milne to LMS Directors, Malacca, December 30, 1815, Special Archive and Collection, CWM/LMS/14/02/01/008, SOAS Library, London.
William Milne to LMS Directors, Malacca, October 23, 1816, Special Archive and Collection, CWM/LMS/14/02/01/021, SOAS Library, London.
William Milne to LMS Directors, Malacca, December 31, 1816, Special Archive and Collection, CWM/LMS/14/02/01/022, SOAS Library, London.
William Milne to LMS Directors, Malacca, June 22, 1817, Special Archive and Collection, CWM/LMS/UG/MA/01/02/B, SOAS Library, London.
Withngton, H. *Old Parochial Reg[listers] County Aberdeen Par[ish] Kennethmount*. Vol 212/1. New Register House Edinburgh. 12, 02C186. Edinburgh: Genealogical Society, 1978.
Williams, S. Wells. *The Middle Kingdom; A Survey of the Geography, Government, Education, Social Life, Arts, Religion, &c., of the Chinese Empire and Its Inhabitants*. 2:290–380. London: Wiley and Putnam, 1848.
Wong, Man Kong. "British Missionaries' Approaches to Modern China, 1807–1966." Seventh Special Session of the 19th International Congress of Historical Sciences, Oslo University, Oslo, Norway, August 6–13, 2000.
Wong, Timothy Man-kong. "Milne, Rachel (Cowie)." In *Biographical Dictionary of Christian Missions*, edited by Gerald H. Anderson, 461. Grand Rapids: Eerdmans, 1998.
Wright, Eric E. *A Practical Theology of Missions: Dispelling the Mystery; Rediscovering the Passion*. Leominster, England: Day One, 2010.
Wylie, Alexander. *Memorials of Protestant Missionaries To the Chinese: Giving A List of Their Publications, and Obituary Notices of the Deceased; With Copious Indexes*. Shanghai: American Presbyterian Mission, 1867.
Xiong, Yuezhi. *The Dissemination of Western Learning and the Late Qing Dynasty* "西學東漸與晚清社會." Shanghai: People's Publishing, 1995.
Yang, C. K. *Religion in Chinese Society: A Study of Contemporary Social Functions of Religion and Some of Their Historical Factors*. Berkeley, CA: University of California Press, 1966.
Yeung, Timothy Yiu-Wai. "An Introduction to the Theology of Robert Morrison." *Journal of China Graduate School of Theology* 42 (2007) 81–108.
Ying, Fuk-tsang. "Evangelist At the Gate: An Inquiry Into Robert Morrison's Mission Thought." *Journal of China Graduate School of Theology* 42 (2007) 13–49.

Bibliography

Young, Doyle L. "Andrew Fuller and the Modern Mission Movement." *Baptist History and Heritage* 17.4 (1982) 17–27.

Young, Richard Fox, and Jonathan A. Seitz, eds. *Asia in the Making of Christianity: Conversion, Agency, and Indigeneity, 1600s to the Present.* Leiden, Netherlands: Brill, 2013.

Zheng, Yangwen. *The Social Life of Opium in China.* Cambridge: Cambridge University Press, 2005.

www.ingramcontent.com/pod-product-compliance
Lightning Source LLC
Chambersburg PA
CBHW072152160426
43197CB00012B/2357